MW01156892

arabic
with ease

Day by day method

arabic
with ease

Volume 1

Original Text by

J.J. Schmidt

Adapted for the use of English-speaking readers,
with an Introduction to the language, by

STEPHEN GEIST

Illustration by J.L. GOUSSE

ASSIMIL S.A.

13, rue Gay-Lussac
94430 CHENNEVIERES s/MARNE
FRANCE

Benelux - Düsseldorf - Lausanne - London -
Madrid - Montréal - New York - Torino

"ASSIMIL" METHOD BOOKS

Bound books, lavishly illustrated, containing lessons recorded on records, tapes or cassettes

— — — —

French with ease
Using French
German without toil
Italian without toil
Russian without toil
Spanish without toil

— — — —

© ASSIMIL 1979   Nº ISBN : 2-7005-0087-3

FOREWORD

The aim of this book is to make accessible to English-speaking readers with no special linguistic training, in as simple and pleasant a way as possible, and in the shortest possible time, a language that is spoken by some hundred million people in all parts of the world.

Like the other ASSIMIL language books, this one is meant primarily for people who want (or who are obliged) to learn the language without help from a teacher.

However, as no one can learn by himself exactly how to *pronounce* an unfamiliar foreign language, whether Arabic or French, we recommend to our readers that, unless they have Arabic-speaking friends, they make use, along with the book, of the ASSIMIL recording of the complete course (available both on records and in cassettes), in which the sentences of every Lesson are spoken aloud.

The ASSIMIL method is based on a practical step-by-step initiation into the language, not on rules of grammar. People whose native language is English are usually impatient with grammar as such. The question that interests them, when they learn a foreign language, is not, "What are the rules ?" but **"How does it work ?"** It is to this question that we always try to give the answer.

Many kinds of Arabic are used in the Arab world. The kind that concerns us in this book is what might be called **modern international Arabic** — the written and spoken language used by literate people from all parts of the Arab world to communicate with one another. It is the language of newspapers, of correspondance, of business, of radio, of television, of international relations, of public notices, of street signs. It is understood by virtually everyone ; and with it you can make your way around anywhere in the Arab world, whether in Marrakech or in Kuwait.

This book is intended for English-speaking readers everywhere. We hope our British readers will not take it amiss that we have tended, when a choice was necessary, to favor American spellings and usages (*color* for *colour, baggage* for *luggage, will* for *shall* in most instances, and so on).

The present volume, written for adult beginners, will be followed by a second one at a more advanced level.

WHAT IS IN THIS BOOK AND HOW TO USE IT

The book starts with a general **INTRODUCTION**, in which we explain the letters of the alphabet and their sounds, how Arabic is written, how Arabic words are formed, and how words are put together to make Arabic sentences (which are often very unlike sentences in English). We suggest that you read the Introduction with great care. Any time that you "lose" doing so you will regain many times over by the end of the first few lessons.

The book ends with an **INDEX**, which will enable you to refer back at any time to details that you are not sure of or that you don't remember where to find.

Between the Introduction and the Index the book consists of **42 LESSONS**, which theoretically correspond to 42 days. These are organized in groups of six, followed by a seventh which reviews the most important (or the most troublesome) points covered in them. It is unlikely that you will be able to respect the seven-day work week that we have in mind, but this is of no importance.

The individual Lessons are made up of some or all of the following ingredients :

(a) **Sentences.** These are based on everyday words and situations. Each sentence is first printed in Arabic script. Underneath or opposite the Arabic, we show, by a very simple method of transcription, how to pronounce it. Under the pronunciation, we translate the sentence into its more or less colloquial English equivalent, indicating by parentheses words that, in literal translation, are added or left out or placed in a different order. This procedure will soon familiarize you with specifically Arabic ways of saying things. Use the translation of each sentence as a guide to its meaning ; but learn as quickly as possible *to think and to feel the sentence in Arabic.*

(b) **Notes.** Whenever a word or a turn of phrase in a sentence brings up a point that needs to be explained, you are referred by a number in parentheses to a correspondingly numbered Note on it. Problems are dealt with one by one, as they arise, not in bulk packages, so that you make your way into them gradually.

(c) **Exercises.** in reading, writing and speaking, based on the contents of the Lesson.

(d) **Grammar,** such as the conjugation of verbs, in limited doses, and again as the need for it arises. Both in these special grammatical sections and in the Notes, grammar is dealt with in a very simplified (in fact over-simplified) way. Our object is not to make you a grammarian but to give you a good practical grasp of how the language "works".

(e) **Comments,** which we insert whenever we think they will be helpful, to show you where you are and where you are going, or to explain more fully than in the Notes matters that may puzzle you.

Study carefully each sentence of the day's Lesson, with its pronunciation and its translation, referring to the explanatory Notes as you come to them. Then re-read all the sentences of the Lesson aloud (imitating as closely as possible the way they are pronounced in the recording, if you have it). Repetition will familiarize you quickly with the sound of Arabic ; and you will acquire with surprising speed a "feel" for the special ways in which Arabic sentences are formed. You will at first passively absorb the Lessons, then assimilate them, and finally be able to make active use of them.

You will of course have to work at this. It would be foolish to pretend that Arabic or any other foreign language can be learned without effort. And you will have to work at it regularly, so that the full benefit of every lesson carries over into the next and creates its own momentum. But the ASSIMIL method is designed to make the effort as interesting and painless as any effort can be, as well as self-rewarding : you learn as you move along, you move along as you learn.

INTRODUCTION

A. Arabic letters, sounds and signs

1 Letters having familiar sounds
2 Letters whose sounds are not familiar
3 Long vowels
4 Short vowels
5 Diphthongs
6 Missing sounds
7 Special forms of letters
8 Special signs

B. The Arabic alphabet, how it is written, and how words are made from it.

1 Preliminary remarks
2 Table of the Arabic alphabet in all its forms
3 How to write Arabic letters
4 Easy-to-recognize Arabic words

C. The internal structure of Arabic words

D. How sentences are formed from words

1 Parts of speech
2 Nouns
3 Verbs

INTRODUCTION

A. Arabic letters, sounds and signs

The Arabic alphabet, like the alphabets of all Semitic languages, in no way resembles those of English and of the European languages, though many of its letters correspond to similar sounds. It must be learned as you learned the English alphabet when you were a child. This is not nearly so difficult as it at first appears, and you will be pleasantly surprised at how quickly, with practice, you master it.

The biggest stumbling block in the way of learning to read Arabic script is the difficulty that a learner has, in most books written for him, in distinguishing the letters themselves. We therefore start by showing them to you in large, clear type. This will enable you to grasp the exact shape of each letter and how to form it, so you will not jump to the usual conclusion that Arabic writing is a hopeless jumble of curlicues.

Throughout this book — both as a walking-stick for diligent learners and as an artificial leg for less diligent ones — we use a simple method of representing the sounds of all but one of the letters of the Arabic alphabet by letters of the English alphabet. (You don't have to learn phonetics in addition to Arabic). You could in fact go through the complete series of lessons without learning the Arabic alphabet at all. But we strongly advise you not to take this easy way out, if only because you will want, in the Arab countries, to read the names of streets and the No Smoking signs, to distinguish a bookshop from a bakery, and to have at least a rough idea of what is in the newspapers.

Although Arabic letters are formed differently from English letters, they have the advantage, once you know them, of representing one and *only one* sound. There is no such problem as the one that has to be dealt with by a foreigner learning English when he comes to a phrase such as : "... Though still coughing, she bought at a bookshop near the old watering trough in Slough a novel by Meredith ; she went through it from cover to cover, but found it rough going" (G. Sczeyn). (Take a bough, young lady, and another one if you could handle Slough.)

We will move into Arab letters, sounds and signs by stages :

1 Letters having familiar sounds. About three fifths of the 29 letters in the Arabic alphabet have sounds that are very much like those of equivalent letters in English (or in common European languages that you have certainly heard spoken). All 29 are considered to be consonants, but three of these also act as long vowels and are called vowel-consonants. In the following table, we will start with the "pure" consonants, then go on to the vowels. (At the head of the table, the abbreviation "Tran." means the letter or group of letters by which we transcribe the Arabic sound.)

Letter	Tran.	Name	Pronunciation
ب	b	baa'	**b**un, **b**ar
ت	t	taa'	**t**ot, **t**oot
ث	th	thaa'	**th**ink, **th**ump
ج	j	jeem	**j**am, **j**ump
خ	kh	khaa'	Scottish lo**ch**, German a**ch**
د	d	daal	**d**u**d**, **d**i**d**
ذ	dh	dhaal	**th**is, **th**us
ر	r	raa'	rolled Scottish bu**rr**ow
ز	z	zeen	**z**ero, **z**ig**z**ag
س	s	seen	**s**i**s**ter, **s**ad
ش	sh	sheen	**sh**oot, **sh**ush
ف	f	faa'	**f**ool, **f**un
ك	k	kaaf	**K**odak, **k**angaroo
ل	l	laam	**l**uck, **l**oud
م	m	meem	**m**oon, **m**ouse
ن	n	noon	**n**oon, **n**un
ه - ه	h	haa'	**h**at, **h**ip [pronounced wherever it occurs in a word, even at the end]

2 Letters whose sounds are not familiar. A number of other letters, characteristically Semitic, have no equivalent sounds in English. These sounds can not be properly described : they must be listened to and imitated. In general, they are sounds made either from far back in the throat or with the tongue in such a position as to make the palate cavernous. You will have trouble with them at first ; but you will master them, with practise, in a reasonable time.

The first four of these letters, with dots under them in our transcription, are called "emphatics". They are basically similar to the English letters by which we represent them, BUT pronounced as if you had a doctor's spoon on your tongue or a hot potato in front of your mouth. Consider the dots to represent hot potatoes. Practise pronouncing them *along with* one of the Arabic vowels (it is practically impossible to pronounce them *without* a vowel). You will see at once that, because of the way you have to shape the inside of your mouth to pronounce them, they *change* the vowel sounds, so that **aa**, for example, becomes something like the **aw** in "awful".

ص	ṣ	saad	See remarks above
ض	ḍ	daad	
ط	ṭ	taa'	
ظ	ẓ	zaa'	

The next four letters, arranged in order of increasing strangeness, are all pronounced from far back in the throat with air expelled from the chest. The first, which is the least difficult, is like a very harsh, throaty h. (Although it is not one of the "emphatics", we show it too with a dot under it, for lack of any other way to differentiate it from a straighforward **h**.) The second one, which we represent by **q**, has the sound of a **k** pronounced from the throat rather than from the palate. (The distinction between **q** and **k** is essential.) The third, **gh**, somewhat resembles a Parisian **r** as pronounced by Maurice Chevalier or Charles Boyer, but rougher, like a clearing of the throat. And the last, which is almost a gagging sound, is so remote from anything in English that we do not try to represent it by anything but itself.

ح	**h**	haa'	See remarks above
ق	**q**	qaaf	
غ	**gh**	ghain	
ع	ε	εain	

The twenty-ninth letter (which is often considered to be a sign rather than a letter) will suggest to you rather a suspension of sound than a sound in itself. We represent it in transcription as an apostrophe.

ء	'	hamza

As you will see a great deal of *hamza,* we will say a few words here about how it is pronounced and more later about how it is used. Officially it is called a "glottal stop" ; its name means "the digging in of a spur" ; it corresponds to what happens in your throat in the middle of "trick key" or "big hog". It is generally compared to the missing sound in the Cockney pronunciation of "butter" : "bu'er". But it occurs as often as not at the *beginning* of Arabic words ; and this takes a li'l doing.

3 Long vowels. We have said that three of the 29 letters of the Arabic alphabet are also used as vowels. They are the *only* three vowels that are used in *written* Arabic. All three have familiar English sounds ; and all are, in principle, long vowels ; but in fact, *when they are used at the end of a word, they are pronounced short,* and we show them that way in our transcription. (We have the same thing in English : think of the long-and-short "ee" sounds in "merely" or "meaty".) Two of these long vowels serve also as consonants, in the same way as the similar English vowel-consonants w and y.

و	oo	waw	food, moon
	w		water, wind
ا	aa	'alif	Baa, baa, black sheep
ي	ee	yaa'	eel, peel
	y		yoyo, yes

You will see shortly why we list the three long vowels in this particular order.

4 Short vowels. Three short vowels are also used in *spoken* Arabic, but they are not normally written ; and they are not considered to be letters of the alphabet. The sounds of all three are again familiar to you : they are shortened or "flattened" versions of the long vowels. "Food" becomes "foot", whose sound we represent, for clarity, by the u of "put". The long aa of "Baa, baa, black sheep" becomes the short a of "Ta-ta, see you soon." And "peel" becomes "pill". When spoken, these short vowels tend to blur and to be absorbed into the consonants, that go with them ; or they flatten out to somewhat neutral sounds like the u in "bug" or the e in "the".

If the short vowels are not normally written

(except in editions of the Coran, in some dictionaries and in books for beginners), how can you recognize them ? You are simply expected to know that they *ought* to be there from your recognition of the words themselves in their context, as you do in English when, for example, the personal shorthand in which you take notes, records "capital required" as "cptl rqrd". As we do not expect from you, in the learning stage, any such exploit, we transcribe all the short vowel sounds.

When, in Arabic script, the short vowels *are* written, they are not written as letters but as small strokes, straight or twisted, placed under or over the consonants that precede them, as we show below, using the consonant "d" to illustrate.

For reasons that we will explain in a moment, the short vowels often have an **n** sound added to them. (This is called "nunation", but we will avoid using this grammatical term, like most others.) The addition of the "n" sound is represented by a small change in the sign that represents the short vowel itself.

Here, then, are the three short vowels (preceded by "d" to illustrate), with and without "n" after them :

دُ	du	damma	With n :	دٌ	d**un**
دَ	da	fat-ha	With n :	دًا	d**an**
دِ	di	kasra	With n :	دٍ	d**in**

Now we come to a tricky but important point related to short vowels. As the signs that represent them are not letters of the alphabet, they can not stand on their own feet : they have to be *carried by* a consonant. When the short vowel comes *after* the consonant, as in **du, da** and **di** above, this is no problem. But when, at the beginning of a word, it comes *before* the consonant, as in **ud, ad** and **id,** it needs something to carry it. The job of carrier is done by the letter **'alif**, *which in this situation has no sound at all* : it serves merely as the inert "carrier" of the short vowel sign, which either sits on it (**u** and **a**) or hangs from it (**i**).

But we can not in fact write **ud**, **ad** and **id** as such : *Arabic words can not begin with a vowel.* So a consonant has to be inserted before the vowel. The consonant used for this purpose is the "soundless" **hamza**, which is itself carried by the inert **'alif** along with the vowel, giving (in transcription) **'ud**, **'ad** and **'id** — and such words as **'al**, **'alif**, **'ahmad**.

5 Diphthongs. In Arabic, as in English, when the sound **aa** is combined with the sound **ee** it makes a diphthong having the sound of **aa-ee**. The simplest way to represent this sound is by **ay**.

The only other diphthong you will encounter in Arabic is the equally familiar combination of **aa** with **oo**, as in "now". To avoid confusion with other sounds, we represent this by **aw**.

6 Missing sounds. A certain number of common English sounds *do not exist at all* in Arabic. So when words are borrowed by Arabic from English (or from other languages), they have to be "twisted", both in speaking and in writing, to the means at its disposal. This is not always easy ; and there is always a risk of confusion. Here are some examples :

Missing sound	Replaced by	Example
v	**f**	television - tilifisioon
p	**b**	petrol(eum) - bitrool
hard **g**	**gh**	gas - ghaaz
the **a** and	**aa**	radio - raadiooo
the **o** of radio	**oo**	

For another example of the problems created by missing sounds, see page 26, Note 4.

7 Special forms of letters. There are just a couple of these, and they present no problem :

Letter	Tran.	Name	Explanation
لا	la	—	Just a convenient combination of l plus a.
ة ـة	t	taa' marboota	The name means "looped t". It is a special form of t, in two versions, unattached and attached, identical with the Arabic h, but with a pair of dots added. (There are historical reasons for this, but we can skip them for now.) At the end of a word, the **taa' marboota** identifies the word as a feminine singular. It is not usually pronounced unless it is followed by a vowel that is likewise pronounced. But vowels at the end of words are rarely pronounced in everyday speech, unless they are needed as "bridges" to a word or syllable that follows. This is why you will most often see the taa' marboota endings transcribed in parentheses : (tu) (ta) (ti).

8 Special signs. These are, among other things, guides to pronunciation. You will need to know them in order to read directly from Arabic script.

Sign	Tran.	Name	Explanation
°	—	sukoon	Its name means "silence". It is placed over every conso-

XVII

			nant that has no vowel after it.
ـّ	—	shadda	This sign written over a consonant doubles it. A single f with shadda over it becomes ff, which is how we show it in transcription. Pronounce it as a *sustained* letter, not as "fuf" or as "f'f". *Hold* all double letters as if you were explaining to a child : "This is ffff ; this is llll..."
ء	´	hamza	We have already seen that this may be considered a consonant ; but we will come back to it now say more about how it is used. As a consonant it may stand alone ; but it is most often *carried by* (and *written over*) one of the long vowels, **oo, aa** or **ee**. At the beginning of a word, its "bearer" is always **aa** (**'alif**). In the course of the lessons, you will see it written in various ways.
آ	'aa	madda	This is just **hamza** plus **aa**.

B. The Arabic alphabet, how it is written and how words are made from it.

1 Preliminary remarks.

Now that we have seen the individual letters that make up the alphabet, their sounds and the signs that are used with them, we will look at the alphabet as a whole, in its customary order, and at how Arabic letters and words are written. A few preliminary remarks are needed :

(a) Like all the Semitic languages, Arabic is written from **right to left** (a boon for the left-handed). You will quickly discover that this is almost as natural as writing from left to right. (And Arabic books are read **from back to front** — a *more* natural way, as any magazine reader knows, than going from front to back.)

(b) There is no difference, in Arabic, between the printed and the handwritten form of a letter ; and there are no capitals. So you don't have to learn, as you do in English, four different ways of reading and writing the same letter, such as R, r and the longhand versions of R and r.

(c) But things are not quite so simple. Although each Arabic letter does have just one basic shape when it stands alone, the basic shape of many letters undergoes certain changes — always the same ones for each letter — depending on whether the letter stands at the **beginning** of a word, in the **middle,** or at the **end.** At the beginning of a word, much of the basic shape tends to be chopped off ; in the middle, it tends to be simplified or elongated so that it can more easily be joined to the letters before and after it ; and, at the end of a word, it is likely to have a final flourish, like the signature of an important businessman.

On the following pages, you will find a complete table of the Arabic letters in alphabetical order, showing all the changes of shape that they undergo, with their transcribed sounds and with examples of their use in words. Notice that **certain letters,** marked with an asterisk, **can not be attached to the letters which follow them.** Notice also that the table is set up to be read from right to left.

TABLE OF THE ARABIC ALPHABET IN ALL ITS FORMS
with transcribed sounds and examples

Note : Letters marked with ★ are never attached to letters that follow

At end of word	In middle of word	At beginning of word	Alone
ء ماء water maa'	ء كأس glass ka's	ء الولد child 'al walad	ء = ا ★
ـا عصا stick ᵉasa	ا قال he said qaala	ا ابي my father 'abi	ا = aa ★
ـب ذهب he went dhahaba	ـبـ قبل before qabla	بـ باب door baab	ب = b
ـت أنت you 'anta	ـتـ يتكلم he speaks yatakallam	تـ تعال come ! taᵉaala	ت = t

At end of word	In middle of word	At beginning of word	Alone
ثالث third thaalith	مثل like mithla	ثمّ then thumma	ث = th
خروج exit khurooj	يجلس he sits yajlis	جميل handsome jameel	ج = j
فرح joy farah	تحت under tahta	حتّى until hatta	ح = H
صرخ he shouted sarakha	بخشيش tip bakhsheesh	خبز bread khoubz	خ = kh
ولد child walad	أبداً never 'abadan	دار house daar	د = d

At end of word	In middle of word	At beginning of word	Alone
ك	ك	ك	ذ = dh *
take! khudh	this haadha	that dhaalik	
			ر = t
wine khamr	cold bard	man rajul	
			ز = z *
rice ruzz	he came down nazala	he visited zaara	
			س = s
sun shams	happy masroor	gentleman sayyidi	
			ش = sh
thirst ᶜatash	drinks mashroobaat	he drank shariba	

At end of word	In middle of word	At beginning of word	Alone
cheap rakhees·	we arrive nasil	morning sabaah·	s· =
some baεd·	correct madboot·	noise dajeej	d· =
only faqat·	airport mataar	airplane taa'ira·	t· =
he kept hafiza	big εazeem	darkness zalaam	z· =
with maεa	after baεda	on εala	ε =

At end of word	In middle of word	At beginning of word	Alone
empty faarigh	small ṣagheer	tomorrow ghadan	ع = gh
thousand 'alf	infant ṭifl	girl fataat	ف = f
friend ṣadeeq	name laqab	heart qalb	ق = q
on you ᵉalayk	he speaks yatakallam	book kitaab	ك = k
moreover bal	money fuloos	why? limaadha	ل = l

At end of word	In middle of word	At beginning of word	Alone
mouth fam	I slept nimtu	key miftaah	م = m
the right 'al yameen	he forgets yansa	window naafidha	ن = n
this [fem.] haadhihi	I understood fahimtu	this [masc.] haadha	ه = h
if law	beans fool	and wa	و = w
tea shaay	sir sayyid	he comes down yanzil	ي = y

3 How to write Arabic letters. The easiest and most effective way to learn how to write (as well as how to read) Arabic letters is to trace or copy them. But you will probably be in some doubt about the way in which your pen should move in order to form them properly. So as to settle this matter once and for all, we give you a second time, on the following pages, a complete table of the Arabic alphabet, showing this time exactly how your pen should move to form each letter. We suggest that you use this table as a basis for copying-exercises on a larger scale than the format of this book allows. We again give you the transcribed sound of each letter ; and we again indicate by an asterisk the letters that can not be joined to letters which follow them.

HOW TO WRITE ARABIC LETTERS

	Alone	At beginning	In middle	At end of word
hamza *	ء hamza	ٵ or ء or ٸ	ٵ or ٸ or ٴ or ٸ	ء or ٸ or ٵ
a *	ا →	ا →	ا or ـا	ـا
b	ب	ب	ـبـ	ـب or ـب or ب
t	ت	ت	ـتـ	ـت
th	ث	ث	ـثـ	ـث

XXVII

HOW TO WRITE ARABIC LETTERS

	Alone	At beginning	In middle	At end of word
j				
ḥ •				
kh				
d *				
dh *				

HOW TO WRITE ARABIC LETTERS

	At end of word	In middle	At beginning	Alone	
					r
					*
					z
					*
					s
					sh
					s.

XXIX

HOW TO WRITE ARABIC LETTERS

	Alone	At beginning	In middle	At end of word
d	ضمــ ضـر	ضـ ضـ	ـضـ ـضـر	ـض ـضـر
t	ط طـ	طـ طـ	ـط ـطـ	ـط ـطـ
z	ظ ظـ	ظـ ظـ	ـظـ ـظـ	ـظ ـظـ
ᶜ	ع عـ	عـ عـ	ـعـ ـعـ	ع عـ or عـ
gh	غ غـ	غـ غـ	ـغـ ـغـ	غ غـ or غـ

HOW TO WRITE ARABIC LETTERS

At end of word		In middle	At beginning	Alone	
					f
	or				q
	or				k
	or				l
	or				m

HOW TO WRITE ARABIC LETTERS

At end of word		In middle		At beginning		Alone	
							n
							h
							w *
							y

4 Easy-to-recognize Arabic words. We introduced in the table of the Arabic alphabet, to illustrate the use of the letters, a certain number of common Arabic words ; and you have certainly begun to grasp how letters are combined in Arabic script to form words. So that you will feel more at ease with them before you go on to the lessons, and so that you may easily practise pronouncing and copying (or tracing) them, we have set up on the following pages a list of Arabic words which, in most cases, you will easily recognize. Some are native Arabic words which have been absorbed into English and French ; some are English and French words that have been absorbed into Arabic.

The Arabic script is written, as is customary, without short-vowel signs. But our transcriptions show where they are and what they are.

We will take the probably unnecessary precaution of reminding you, for the last time, that Arabic is read and written from **right to left.**

Finally, you will want to know where to put the **stresses** when pronouncing words. Arabic is a strongly rhythmical language. The rhythm, however, is given not by any such system of "tonic accents" as we have in English but by the fact that **long vowels are held longer** than other sounds and thus automatically receive the stress. When there is more than one long vowel in a word, put the stress on the one that is closest to the end of it. This is the only rule to remember. If you hold the long vowels and keep the short ones short, you will come out right every time.

English	Transcription	Arabic
cotton	qutn	قطن
wadi (river bed)	waad	واد
caliph	khaleefa	خليفة
Mahdi	mahdi	مهدي
sugar	sukkar	سكّر
papa, pope	baaba	بابا
Damascus	dimashq	دمشق
minaret	manaara	منارة
soap (French : *savon*)	saaboon	صابون
naphta	naft	نفط
souk (Arab market)	sooq	سوق
algebra	'al-jabr	ألجبر
emirate	'imaara	إمارة
Beirut	bayroot	بيروت
Koran	qur'aan	قرأن
cipher (zero)	sifr	صفر
sultan	sultaan	سلطان
mechanic	meekaaneeka	ميكانيكا
Medina	'al madeena	ألمدينة

English	Transcription	Arabic
bank	bank	بنك
dinar	deenaar	دينار
dirham (currency)	dirham	درهم
felsite (rock)	fals	فلس
France	faransa	فرنسا
salaam (peace)	salaam	سلام
technology	tiknooloojiya	تكنولوجيا
diplomacy	dibloomaasiyya	دبلوماسيّة
vizir	wazeer	وزير
emir	'ameer	أمير
Jack	jaak	جاك
bakshich (tip)	bakhsheesh	بخشيش
baraka (English charisma)	baraka	بركة
Leila	layla	ليلى
Mohammed	muḥammad	محمّد
petrol	bitrool	بترول
Arabic	$^\epsilon$arabi	عربيّ
French	faransi	فرنسيّة
Baghdad	baghdaad	بغداد

English	Transcription	Arabic
petrochemistry	bitrookeemiyaa'	بتروكيمياء
Tunis	toonis	تونس
franc	farank	فرنك
magasin (French for *store*)	makhzan	مخزن
plastic	blaasteek	بلاستيك
Moslem	muslim	مسلم
Islam	'islaam	إسلام
Allah	'allaah	الله
goudron (French for *tar*)	qaṭiraan	قطران
gas	ghaaz	غاز
geography	jughraafiya	جغرافيا
hydrogen	haydroojeen	هيدروجين
electronics	'iliktrooneek	إلكترونيك
toubib (French slang for *doctor*)	ṭabeeb	طبيب
Paris	baarees	باريس
Libya	leebya	ليبيا
Omar	ᶜumar	عمر
check	sheek	شيك
sheikh	shaykh	شيخ

English	Transcription	Arabic
Aden, Eden	ᶜadn	عدن
Cairo	'al qaahira	ألقاهرة
Raïs	ra'ees	رئيس
kilogram	keelooghraam	كيلوغرام
kilometer	keeloomitr	كيلومتر
centime	santeem	سنتيم
Iraq	'al ᶜiraaq	ألعراق
taxi	taaksi	تاكسي
dynamics	deenaarneeka	ديناميكا
Atlas	'al 'aṭlas	ألأطلس
gazelle	ghazaal	غزال
Sahara	'aṣ-ṣaḥraa'	ألصّحراء
Rabat	'ar-ribaaṭ	ألرّباط
caïd (french slang for crime boss)	qaa'id	قائد
Kaaba	'al kaᶜba	ألكعبة
Mecca	makka	مكّة
muezzin	mu'adhdhin	مؤذّن
Hegira	'al hijra	ألهجرة
chemistry	keemyaa'	كيمياء

XXXVII

English	Transcription	Arabic
Amman	ᵉammaan	عمّان
Riyadh	'ar-ryaaḍ	أَلرّياض
Sanaa	ṣanᵉaa'	صنعاء
Algiers (or *Algeria*)	'al jazaa'ir	ألجزائر
turf, peat	turb	ترب
Abdullah	ᵉabdullaah	عبد الله
Abdel Krim	ᵉabdul kareem	عبد الكريم
Salim	saalim	سالم
Solomon	sulaymaan	سليمان
television	tilifizyoon	تلفزيون
radio	raadyoo	راديو
physics	feezyaa'	فيزياء
Ramadan (fasting month)	ramaḍaan	رمضان
mean (French mesquin)	miskeen	مسكين
city, country (bled is French slang for "hick town")	balad	بلد

C. The internal structure of Arabic words

English words, in their non-compounded forms, are complete units in themselves, each of which has its own history **as a word**. We will take as examples the words **book, write, desk, office, clerk, letter**. These are basic units from which we can make various compounds (bookshop, bookshelf, etc.). They have a certain "conceptual" relation among themselves — they all have to do, in one way or another, with the act of writing — but they are wholly unrelated *words,* each with its own history.

Arabic words are formed in a quite different way. All the words in Arabic corresponding to the ones that we have given above in English belong to a single "family" whose common ancestor is *the concept itself of writing.* This concept is expressed by a so-called **ROOT** made up of three consonants, in this instance **K-T-B**. By adding to this consonant root one or another combination of vowels in one or another order, called a **PATTERN**, we obtain various specific words related to the concept of writing, as well as various shades of meaning among them. Thus **kitaab** is "a book", **'uktub** is "Write!", **maktab** is "an office" and so on.

As this is a basic principle of the Arabic language which it is essential that you grasp from the start, we will insist upon it now and show with a few examples how the principle works. (In the course of the Lessons we will call your attention to it from time to time, particularly by identifying the roots of verbs as we encounter them.)

We will first take two different 3-consonant **ROOTS** to which various vowel patterns give a range of specific meanings within a general conceptual family.

1 Root J-M-$^\epsilon$ ("togetherness")

JaMa$^\epsilon$a	He gathered together, added up, collected
JaM$^\epsilon$	A gathering, a sum
JaM$^\epsilon$iyya	Club, association, league
JaaMi$^\epsilon$a	University
JuM$^\epsilon$a	Friday (the day of gathering together)
JaaMi$^\epsilon$	Great mosque (the place of gathering together)
JaMee$^\epsilon$	Whole (what is gathered together)
muJtaMa$^\epsilon$	Society
'iJMaa$^\epsilon$	Unanimity, concensus
muJaMMi$^\epsilon$	Collector (technical), accumulator (battery)

2 Root $^\epsilon$-L-M ("knowing")

$^\epsilon$aLiMa	He knew
$^\epsilon$aLLaMa	He taught
'a$^\epsilon$LaMa	He informed
ta$^\epsilon$aLLaMa	He learned
'ista$^\epsilon$LaMa	He gathered information
$^\epsilon$iLM	Science
$^\epsilon$uLooM	Sciences
$^\epsilon$iLMi	Scientific
ta$^\epsilon$LeeM	Teaching
ta$^\epsilon$aLLuM	Learning
mu$^\epsilon$aLLiM	Teacher

Now we will take a vowel **PATTERN** and see how it acts in a specific way on a variety of different roots. We will use the pattern **AA-I** ("one who does something").

Root	+ Pattern AA-I	= Word
k-t-b ("writing")	k**AA**t**I**b	One who writes (writer)
ᵉ-m-l ("working")	ᵉ**AA**m**I**l	One who works (work-er)
sh-ᵉ-r ("poetry")	sh**AA**ᵉ**I**r	One who makes poetry (poet)
gh-l-b ("overcoming")	gh**AA**l**I**b	One who overcomes (victor)

As you can at once see, the knowledge of a single root opens the door to a vast number of different words ; and the knowledge of a relatively small number of vowel patterns enables you to identify the specific sense of individual words in a family.

D. How sentences are formed from words

The basic grammatical principles of all the Semitic languages are in many ways different from those of the so-called Indo-European languages, including English. In Arabic, things are not just said in different words from those to which we are accustomed : they are apprehended — thought and felt— in different ways. To learn Arabic is to enter a different world.

What follows is a brief and greatly over-simplified introduction to some special features of Arabic grammar that you will need to know in order to follow the Lessons. (Details will be dealt with in the Lessons themselves as we come to them.) What is involved is the putting together of words and thoughts in unfamiliar ways. This takes some getting used to. But getting used to it is not nearly so difficult as it will at first appear ; and you will soon realize that it is what is most fascinating in the language. Learning Arabic is a bit like learning to swim : different muscles and different muscle movements are needed from those that you use to walk. Our swimming lessons are written for non-swimmers ; and we avoid so far as possible the jargon of grammarians.

1 Parts of speech. The distinctions among "parts of speech" are not nearly so sharp in Arabic as they are in English. Most words are essentially nouns or verbs or offshoots of them. The rest are the miscellaneous nuts, bolts, screws, rivets and pegs with which words are held together to make sentences ; we will call them, as in English, conjunctions ("and", "but", "if") or prepositions ("from", "to", "under") ; but in a few instances, we will have to use the term "particles" for pegs that don't fit anywhere and that have no English equivalents.

Practically all nouns and verbs and their offshoots have **gender** (they are either masculine or feminine) and **number** (singular, plural, or "dual" for two persons or things). The forms of verbs change in accordance with these as well as with **person** (first, second or third). Thus the form of the verb itself in "he said" is different from the one used in "*she* said" ; and "Walk !" is said differently to a man than it is to a woman.

We will deal with these points as we come to them. For the moment we will just quickly summarize Arabic parts of speech, then look more closely at nouns and verbs.

Articles. There is no indefinite article, "a". It is implied in the noun itself. The definite article, "the" — invariable, as in English — is **'al** for both singular and plural words.

Pronouns, as their name indicates, "stand for" nouns. There are two kinds of pronoun : (a) those that **stand alone** as subjects of a verb ("*I* went, "*he* came"), and (b) those that are **attached** to the nouns as possessives ("My wife" becomes in Arabic "wife-my" or "wife-of-me"), or to verbs as their objects ("He hit-me"), or to prepositions as their complements ("from it").

Adjectives, in Arabic, are nouns thinly disguised. "The green houses" becomes "the houses the greens". They agree, in gender and number, with the nouns that they qualify ; and they take the definite article.

Adverbs in Arabic are for the most part nouns used adverbially (that is, in such as way as to say how, when, where, why), as they sometimes are in English : *"Evenings* I am *home"* ; but in Arabic the adverbial function is identified by a special ending, as again it sometimes is in English : "There are departures *daily* and performances *nightly".*

We move on to hybrids that are part noun and part verb.

Participles look verbal (and in English they are), but they behave grammatically in Arabic as if they were adjectives : "I am *enjoying"* is dealt with in much the same way as "I am *grateful".*

Verbal nouns ("the *hunting* of the snark") are exactly what their name says they are. In English we more often call them gerunds.

And we come at last to **verbs** as such, about which we will have more to say in a moment.

As for the miscellaneous odds and ends of linguistic hardware that we spoke of above, it should be mentioned that they are sometimes active parts of the language. As we will see in the course of the Lessons, simple connecting words like "if" and "but" do curious things to the words that come after them, as if they had a life of their own. And connecting words, whether conjunctions or prepositions or particles, are **attached** to the words that follow them when they consist just of a consonant and a short vowel.

2 Nouns

(a) The system of "cases". As we have said, all nouns have **number** (singular or plural or dual) and **gender** (masculine or feminine). But they also have another feature which, if you have never studied a highly inflected language such as German or Latin or Greek, will at first puzzle you : **case.** The word will put you off ; but the idea behind it is fairly simple.

The job a noun does in a sentence, grammatically speaking, is called its "case". There are just three cases, and to each of them corresponds one of the three Arabic short vowels, **-u, -a, -i,** with or without an **-n** sound after it, attached to the end of the noun. If the noun is *definite,* the case-ending is the bare vowel ; if it is *indefinite,* the case-ending is the vowel plus the **-n** sound.

We will explain in a moment what jobs the three cases do. But first, here are their names and the endings they take with definite and indefinite nouns :

	Definite		**Indefinite**	
Subject case	— u	ـُ	— un	ـٌ
Object/adverb case	— a	ـَ	— an	ـاً ـً
Oblique case	— i	ـِ	— in	ـٍ

In the sentence, *"The tree* hides *the man* in *the clearing",* all the nouns are definite, and their case-endings in Arabic will be those of the first column. In its indefinite version, the sentence would read *"A tree* hides *a man* in *a clearing",* and the case-endings would be those of the second column.

In this sentence, "tree" is the **subject** of the verb "hide" and is therefore in the **subject case.** The **object** of the verb "hide" is "man", which is therefore in the **object case.** So far, so good. But why do we call this the object/**adverb** case ? Because very often a noun in this case, instead of completing the sense of the verb by saying *whom* or *what* it acts on, completes it by saying *how, when, where* or *why* it acts, which is the job, in English, of an adverb ("He swims *mornings"*). We will sometimes call this the object case and sometimes the adverb case, depending on the circumstances ; but it is the same case, with the same case-ending.

As for "clearing", in the sentence above, we say that it is in the **oblique case** because it goes off at an angle, so to speak, from the straight line of subject-verb-object. (Some books call it the **indirect case.**) The oblique case, in Arabic, does two specific jobs. The first is to complement (or to be "governed by") a preposition — here the preposition "in". **All prepositions are followed by nouns in the oblique case.** Its second job is to **express "obliquely" the preposition "of"**, in practically all of its many English senses. The "of" is **contained in the oblique case ending ;** there is no separate word for "of" in Arabic.

(b) **Definite and indefinite words.** A noun is "definite" in Arabic, as in English, when it is preceded by "the", but also when it is *made* definite, grammatically speaking, by a word in the oblique case ("of") to which it is joined and that "pins it down". Thus, as you will soon see, the word "a pack", which is obviously *indefinite by nature,* becomes *grammatically definite* (and takes the bare-vowel case ending for definite words) in "a pack **of** cigarettes". We call such combinations of words **yoked couples.** You will find more about them on page 70.

(c) **Plurals.** The plurals of some nouns are formed just by adding plural endings, as in English : "house — houses", "child-children". These are called **external plurals.** But more often the plural is formed by changing the internal structure of the word itself. "A book" is **kitaab ;** "books" is **kutub.** This is called an **internal plural.**

3 Verbs

(a) **Conjugation.** All verbs are "conjugated". That is, their forms change depending on whether their subject is singular or plural or dual, masculine or feminine, and first or second or third person. The changes follow certain fixed schemas which we will look at in the course of the Lessons. As the various forms contain in themselves their implied pronoun subjects (I, you, he, she, etc.), including number and gender, the pronoun need not be expressed separately ; but it *may* be expressed for emphasis : "*You* are swimming, not he".

(b) **Aspects.** Unlike verbs in English, **Arabic verbs have no tenses as such.** That is, they do not relate the action which they express to a particular moment **in time** — past, present or future. They have, instead, **aspects**, which say whether the action expressed is **pending** — that is, not yet completed, and perhaps not yet begun (hence, in a general way, present or future) or **completed**, in fact or in imagination, hence usually (but not always) past.

In its **pending aspect**, the verb "I swim" may mean, depending on its context, "I swim (every Sunday)" or " I am (now) swimming" or "I will swim (next Sunday)" or "I will be swimming (when you arrive)". When the exact sense is not clear from the context, it is made so by various "particles" that we will see as we go along.

As the principle of **aspects** rather than tenses is one of the keys to Arabic grammar, it is essential that you grasp it early.

(c) **Uses of the pending aspect.** A verb in the pending aspect may be used in various ways, all of which you will at once recognize for what they are, though their names may evoke only vague recollections of a time when you had a crush on a plump little girl with pigtails. Depending on the way it is used, the pending aspect of the verb undergoes small changes.

A verb is said to be in the **indicative mood** if it makes a statement : "I **am swimming**" ; "I **swim** like a fish".

It is said to be in the **subjunctive mood** if the action it refers to is subordinate to a verb expressing a wish, a hope, a fear, a command, a need, and so on : "It is important **that I swim**" ; "I want you to **(that you) swim**".

It is said to be **imperative** if it gives an order : "Swim !".

And it is said to be **jussive** if it expresses a wishful half-order that I address to myself, to us, to him, to her or to them : "**May I sink** into the earth if I am not telling the truth ; and **let's learn** from it if we can. **Let** that false friend **swim** till he disappears from sight. As for her, **may** she and all the likes of her **break out** in pimples." (Sulaymaan Bakr)

(d) **Uses of the completed aspect.** In its completed aspect, a verb can have only one mood, the indicative : a statement of a real or imaginary accomplished fact.

(e) **Designation of verbs.** Verbs are designated not by their infinitive ("to swim"), which does not exist in Arabic, but by the third person masculine singular of their completed aspect : "He swam". This is the form in which the root most clearly appears.

(f) **The place of the verb in a sentence.** The verb normally **precedes** its noun-subject in an Arabic sentence. "The Ambassador sings in his bathtub" is written, "Sings the Ambassador in his bathtub".

You should now be well equipped to handle the Lessons that make up the rest of the book.

*   *
 *

Pronounce
'ad-darsu l- 'awwal

الدَّرسُ الأوَّل

في الطّائرة

Pronounce : fi t-taa'ira (ti)
English : In the airplane

١- سيّداتي ، آنساتي ، سادتي ، أهلاً وسهلاً

1 *Pronounce* : sayyidaati, 'aanisaati, saadati, 'ahlan wa sahlan

English : Ladies, young ladies, gentlemen, welcome.

٢- إنتبهوا من فضلِكم !

2 *Pronounce* : 'intabihu, min fadlikum !

English : Your attention, please !

1

٢ـ نرجو منكم عدمُ التّدخيـــن

3 *Pronounce* : narju minkum ᵉadama t-tadkheen

English : You are kindly requested to refrain from smoking (we wish from you no smoking).

٤ـ السّاعةُ الأنَ : ألواحدة بعد الظّهر

4 *Pronounce* : 'as-saaᵉatu l'aan : 'al waaḥida baᵉda z̧-z̧uhr

English : The time (is) now I p.m. (the hour now the one after (the) noon).

٥ـ سنصل في السّادسة مساءً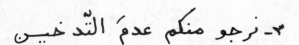

5 *Pronounce* : sanaṣil (1) fi s-saadisa masaa'an

English : We will (1) arrive at 6 p.m. (in the 6th the evening).

٦ـ نتمنّى لكم سفرًا طيّبًا

6 *Pronounce* : natamanna lakum safaran ṭayyiban

English : We wish you a pleasant trip (we wish you trip good).

COMMENTS

1 Your first swimming lesson has consisted of stepping (or jumping) into an unfamiliar medium, water, of learning what it feels like, and of discovering that you can float. Don't take it to heart that you can't yet do the crawl.

2 To derive the most benefit from this and the following lessons :

(a) **Repeat** each sentence aloud several times over, listening to the sound of your own voice — or, better, to that of the voice in the recording — until you get the swing of it.

(b) **Copy** (or trace) each sentence — from **right to left**, of course — so that your hand becomes accustomed to forming words in Arabic script and your eye familiar with the visual shapes that correspond to the spoken sounds : a do-it-yourself audio-visual technique that requires no equipment.

3 When pronouncing, be careful to **"hold"** (as you would hold a musical note) the consonants that are identified as being double by the sign ّ called **shadda** شَدَّة , as in *sayyidaati* سَيِّداتي (See Introduction p. XVIII).

4 Be careful also to **lengthen** properly the long vowels (*aa, oo* and *ee*) whenever they occur, **except** at the end of words. Here are some examples, from the numbered sentences of the lesson :

In 1 : sayyid**aa**ti. In 2 : 'intabihu (short because at the end of word). In 3 : t-tadkh**ee**n. In 4 : w**aa**hida. In 5 : mas**aa**'an.

5 You will have noticed the curious construction of Sentence 3. In English, we would say : "We ask you **not to smoke.**" Arabic generally prefers nouns — or verbal equivalents of nouns (gerunds or participles) such as **"no smoking"** — to verbs. You will meet this constantly from now on.

6 In Sentence 4, notice the absence of the verb "is" between the subject and the predicate : "The time (is) now 1 p.m." This is another regular practise in Arabic. We will have more to say about it on page 32 (in the first Review Lesson), which you may want to take a look at in advance. Sentences of this sort are called "noun sentences".

NOTES

1 You will recall from the Introduction (p. XLVII) that the "pending aspect" of a verb covers both the present and the future. We have here the pending aspect of the verb naṣil ; it may mean either "we *are* arriving" or "we *will be* arriving". To give it the specifically future sense, we add to it the prefix **sa**, and it becomes **sanaṣil** سنصل . Sometimes sa is written **sawfa** سوف

MORE COMMENTS

Probably the one word of Arabic you knew before you opened this book was the definite article **'al**, "the" اَلْ ; and you are wondering why, at the top of page 1, we have shown the pronunciation of the word for "the lesson", written الدرس, to be **'ad-darsou** rather than **'al darsou**. The reason is this : When the **l** of **'al** is followed by one of the letters of the alphabet that are called **"sun"** letters — letters thought of as being dominant — the **l** sound of **'al** is in fact "dominated" by and absorbed into them and changes to **their** sound, which is doubled. As the **d** of **darsu** is a "sun" letter, **'al-darsu** becomes **'ad-darsu.**

All other letters are called **"moon"** letters. When **'al** is followed by one of them, the **l** keeps its pronunciation as l. Here is a list of all the **"moon"** letters, along with some typical examples of words starting with them :

a	'al 'ab	the father	الأب
b	'al baab	the door	الباب
j	'al jibaal	the mountains	الجبال
ḥ	'al ḥaqeeba	the suitcase	الحقيبة
kh	'al khaadim	the servant	الخادم

3

ϵ	'al ϵaashir	the tenth	ألعَاشِر
gh	'al ghurfa	the room	ألغرفة
f	'al firaash	the bed	ألفراش
q	'al qamar	the moon	ألقمر
k	'al kitaab	the book	ألكتاب
m	'al miftaah	the key	ألمفتاح
h	'al hudoo'	the calm	ألهدوء
w	'al wusool	the arrival	ألوصول
y	'al yasaar	the left	أليسار

And here are the "sun" letters :

t	'at-taasiϵ	the ninth	التَّاسِع
th	'ath-thaalith	the third	الثَّالِث
d	'ad-dars	the lesson	الدَّرس
dh	'adh-dhahaab	the "going"	الذَّهاب
r	'ar-ruzz	the rice	الرّز
z	'az-zubda	the butter	الزّبدة
s	'as-sayyaara	the car	السَّيارة
sh	'ash-shams	the sun	الشَّمس
s	'as-sadeeq	the friend	الصَّديق
d	'ad-dayf	the guest	الضَّيف
t	'at-taa'ira	the airplane	الطَّائرة
z	'az-zuhr	(the) noon	الظَّهر
l	'al-lugha	the language	اللّغة
n	'an-naas	the people	النَّاس

4

Pronounce
'ad-darsu th-thaani

الدَّرْسُ الثَّاني

Second Lesson
(The lesson the second)

في الطَّائِرَة

Pronounce : fi t-taa'ira (ti)
English : In the airplane

١- هل تريد جريدة،يا سيِّدي ؟

1 'al mudeefa 'ila Jaak	*Pronounce :* hal tureed jareeda, ya sayyidi ?
The stewardess to Jack	*English :* Do you [sing.] want a newspaper, (oh) sir ?

٢- لا ، أفضّل مجلّة.

2 Jaak	*Pronounce :* la, 'ufaḍḍil majalla (tan)
Jack	*English :* No, I prefer a magazine.

٣- تفضّل ①!

3 'al muḍeefa	*Pronounce :* tafaḍḍal (1) !
The stewardess	*English :* Here you are, sir(1) .

٤- شكرًا !

4 Jaak	*Pronounce :* shukran !
Jack	*English :* Thankyou !

5

٥ـ عَفوًا

5 'al-muḍeefa   *Pronounce* : ᶜafwan
The stewardess   *English* : You are welcome.

٦ـ هل عندكم© سجايـر ؟

6 Jaak   *Pronounce* : hal ᶜindakum (2) sajaayir ?
Jack   *English* : Have you [plural] (2) (any) cigarettes ?

٧ـ نعم ، يـا سيّدي .

7 'al muḍeefa   *Pronounce* : naᶜam, ya sayyidi
The stewardess   *English* : Yes, sir.

٨ـ أعطيني☺علبةؗ⁽⁴⁾ سجايـر

8 Jaak   *Pronounce* : 'aᶜteeni (3) ᶜulbata (4) sajaayir
Jack   *English* : Give me (3) a pack (4) of cigarettes.

٩ـ بكلِّ سرور ؛ ها هي يا سيّدي .

9 'al muḍeefa   *Pronounce* : bi-kulli suroor ; ha hiya, ya sayyidi
The stewardess   *English* : With (all) pleasure ; here it is, sir.

6

NOTES

1 The everyday word **tafaddal** can not be literally translated. It is an all-purpose word that signifies willingness or polite assent. It may mean "here you are" or "all right" or "that's fine" or "go ahead" or "come in" or "sit down" or "please do" or "have one", etc.

2 This harmless looking phrase brings up a number of points that we will just glance at now and discuss more fully later :

(a) **hal** is a sort of verbal question mark that precedes a sentence to make it interrogative.

(b) ^ع**indakum** عند كم , which means "you have" (or, in this instance, "have you ?") is not a verb but a combination of the preposition ^ع**inda** ("at" or "on") with the plural pronoun **kum,** "you". The combination means : "on you—i.e. in your possession—(is)". This is one of several ways that we will see in Arabic of saying "have", in the sense of possession, without using a verb. "I have" becomes : "In my possession (is)" : ^ع**indi** عند ي .

(c) The **kum** in ^ع**indakum** is the **plural** "you". Jack is not asking the hostess whether she personally has any cigarettes but whether "you people" of the airline staff have any. In modern English, we no longer distinguish between the singular "thou" and the plural "you" : we say "you" for both. Arabic, like the European languages, makes this distinction. (It also, as we shall see, has a "you" for two people.) Now and then, in Arabic, the plural "you" is used for a single person when he is of high rank — that is, when in English we would say "Your Excellency" or "Your Honor".

3 The verb "give" أَعْطَى ('a^عta = "he gave"), like similar verbs such as "offer" or "lend", takes two direct objects (the thing given and the person to whom it is given), rather than a direct and an indirect object. "Give the hostess the cigarettes" in Arabic is :

'a^عti l-mudeefa s-sajaayir أَعْطِ المضيفة السّجايَر

4 For reasons that we will momentarily disregard but will discuss in detail later, ^ع**ulbata** ("pack") in the word-combination ^ع**ulbata sajaayir** ("a pack of cigarettes") is considered to be a definite noun even though, in English, it is preceded by the indefinite article "a". As it is the object of the verb "give", it takes the object/adverb case ending -a for definite nouns.

7

Indefinite nouns in the object/adverb case end in **-an**.
This ending is used also for nouns and related words that have an "adverbial" function (i.e., which say how, when, where etc.), as well as for some everyday expressions of adverbial origin :

Tomorrow	**ghadan**	غدًا
In the evening	**masaa'an**	مساءً
Excuse me	**$^\epsilon$afwan**	عفوًا
Thank you	**shukran**	شكرًا
Welcome	**'ahlan wasahlan**	أهلً وسهلً

We will come back to the question of Cases in Review Lesson 7.

For now, we will simply remind you of the following :

(a) In the **subject case, definite nouns** end in **-u**. For example :

The lesson	**'ad-darsu**	الدَّرسُ

Indefinite nouns in the subject case end in **-un**.

(b) In the **oblique case, definite nouns** end in **-i**. When the noun is **indefinite**, **-i** becomes **-in**. In the Arabic expression for "Please" — literally, "out of your grace" — which is **min fadlik** [singular] and **min fadlikum** [plural], you see the oblique case ending **-i**, required by the preposition **min** مِن , plus the attached singular and plural pronouns for "you", **-k** and **-kum**.

The general term "noun" covers words that are assimilated to nouns in Arabic grammar : adjectives, participles ("working") and verbal nouns or gerunds ("the no smoking").

The "rules" given above have certain exceptions that we will point out as we meet them.

هل تريد جريدة
يا سيِّدي ؟

②

8

EXERCISES

ا۔ أعطني جريدة من فضلك

1 'a^ϵtini jareeda min faḍlik

Give [masc. sing.] me a newspaper, please.

٢۔ هل تفضّل سجاير ؟

2 hal tufaḍḍil sajaayir ?

Do you [sing.] prefer cigarettes ?

٣۔ هل تريد جرائد ؟

3 hal tureed jaraa'id ?

Do you [sing.] want (some) newspapers ?

الدّرسُ الثّالث

Pronounce   *English*
'ad-darsu th-thaalith   Third Lesson
    (The lesson the third)

في الطّائرة

Pronounce : fi t-taa'ira (ti)
English : In the airplane

ا۔ يا أنستي، هل عندكم مشروبات؟

1 Jaak   *Pronounce* : ya 'aanisati, hal ^ϵindakum mashroobaat ?

    Jack   *English* : Miss, have you [plur.] anything to drink (any drinks) ?

٢- طبعًا ؛ عندنا عصير فواكه

2 'al muḍeefa   *Pronounce* : ṭabᶜan, ᶜindana ᶜaṣeer fawaakih

The   *English* : Of course, we have fruit juice
stewardess   (juice fruits).

٣- ليمون ، برتقال ، وعندنا ماء معدنيّ

3 'al muḍeefa   *Pronounce* : laymoon, burtuqaal ; wa ᶜindana maa' maᶜdini

The   *English* : Lemon, orange ; we also have
stewardess   (and we have) mineral water.

٤- و شاي و قهوة

4 'al muḍeefa   *Pronounce* : washaay waqahwa

The   *English* : And tea and coffee.
stewardess

٥- أعطيني عصير ليمون

5 Jaak   *Pronounce* : 'aᶜteeni ᶜaṣeer laymoon

Jack   *English* : Give me (a) lemon juice (juice lemon).

٦- و أنت ، يا سيّدي ، ماذا تأخذ ؟

6 'al muḍeefa   *Pronounce* : wa'anta, ya sayyidi maadha
'ila jaarihi   ta'khudh ?

The   *English* : And you, sir, what will you have
stewardess   (what do you take) ?
to his neighbor

10

٧ـ أنا أفضّل قهوة بلا سكّر

7 'aḥmad	*Pronounce* : 'ana 'ufaḍḍil qahwa bila sukkar
Ahmad	*English* : I prefer coffee without sugar.

٨ـ هل أنت سائح يا سيّدي ؟

8 Jaak	*Pronounce* : hal 'anta saa'iḥ, ya sayyidi ?
Jack	*English* : (Are) you (a) tourist, sir ?

٩ـ لا، أنا في عطلة

9 'aḥmad	*Pronounce* : la, 'ana fi ᶜuṭla
Ahmad	*English* : No, I (am) on vacation.

١٠ـ و عائد⑤ إلى بلادي ©

10 'aḥmad	*Pronounce* : waᶜaa'id (1) 'ila bilaadi (2)
Ahmad	*English* : And I (am) returning (1) to my country (2).

NOTES

1. When, in English, we refer to a continuing action or state in the present time, we use as a matter of course the so-called "continuous present" tense, made up of a present participle plus the auxiliary "to be" : "*I am going* to the beach" or "*I am feeling* under the weather". The same is true in Arabic, which says, in effect, just as English does : "I am *in the act of going*" or "*in the state of feeling*" ; but in Arabic the connecting auxiliary verb is left out. These so-called active participles are assimilated, as they often are in English, to descriptive adjectives : we say that a woman who exercises charm is "charming", that a book which arouses sentiment is "moving". Here Ahmad is "returning" in much the same way that he might be "intelligent" or "bald" or "knock-kneed".

11

2. The word used here for "country", **bilaad** بلاد بلد is in fact the plural of the word for "town" or "city", **balad** بلد

(Arabic civilization being essentially urban, a country is considered to be a collection of towns.) The plural of the already plural word **bilaad** is **buldaan** بلدان

"The Arab countries", in the plural, may be written in either of two ways :

'al bilaadu l^ϵarabiyya ٱلبلادُ العربيّة

'al buldaanu l^ϵarabiyya ٱلبلدانُ العربيّة

Notice in these examples that, while the nouns **bilaadu** and **buldaanu** are both plurals, the adjective used with them, ^ϵ**arabiyya** is a feminine singular. We will explain why later on.

COMMENTS

Practise pronouncing correctly all the Arabic sounds. You will have a little trouble at first with such specifically Arabic sounds as ع (which we transcribe as ^ϵ and whose name is ^ϵ**ayn**) ; ق (**q**) ; and ح (**ḥ**). But your ear will gradually become accustomed to them, especially if you make use of the recorded lessons.

Pay particular attention to the so-called "emphatic" consonants, which are pronounced from far back in the throat. These "emphatics" are identified in our transcriptions, as we pointed out in our discussion of the alphabet, by the "hot potato" dots under them :

ṭ	ط	in	taa'ira	طائرة
			tayyib	طيّب
			tabeeb	طبيب
			tab^ϵan	طبعًا
ṣ	ص	in	^ϵaseer	عصير
			sahafi	صحفي
ḍ	ض	in	mudeefa	مضيفة

12

EXERCISES

١ـ أنا سائح

1 'ana saa'ih
I (am a) tourist.

٢ـ هل تريد قهوة ؟

2 hal tureed qahwa ?
Do you [sing.] want (some) coffee ?

٣ـ ماذا تفضّل يا سيّدي ؟

3 maadha tufaddil, ya sayyidi ?
What do you prefer, sir ?

٤ـ هل تأخذ عصير ليمون ؟

4 hal ta'khudh ᵋaseer laymoon ?
Do you [sing.] take lemon juice ?

٥ـ سنصل في السّادسة صباحًا

5 sanasil fi s-saadisa sabaahan
We will arrive at 6 a.m. (in the 6th, morning).

٦- هل أنت عائد إلى بلادك؟

6 hal 'anta ᵉaa'id 'ila bilaadik ?

(Are) you returning to your country ?

الدَّرْسُ الرَّابِع

Pronounce
'ad-darsu r-raabiᵉ

English
Fourth Lesson
(The lesson the fourth)

فِي الطَّائِرَة

Pronounce : fi t-taa'ira (ti)

English : In the airplane

١- هل أنت طبيب؟

1 Jaak

Jack

Pronounce : hal 'anta tabeeb ?

English : (Are) you [masc. sing.] (a) doctor ?

٢- لا، أنا معلّم، و أنت؟

2 'aḥmad

Ahmad

Pronounce : la, 'ana muᵉallim ; wa 'anta?

English : No, I (am a) teacher ; and you [sing.] ?

14

٣ـ أَنا صحفيّ

3 Jaak   *Pronounce* : 'ana sahafi

   Jack   *English* : I (am a) journalist.

٤ـ أَه ! طَيّب !

4 'ahmad   *Pronounce* : 'aah ! tayyib !

  Ahmad   *English* : Oh ! How interesting ! (Oh ! Fine !)

٥ـ سامحني ، يا سيّدي ؛ هل معك كبريت ؟

5 Jaak   *Pronounce* : saamihni, ya sayyidi ; hal ma$^\epsilon$ak kibreet ?

   Jack   *English* : Excuse me, sir, have you (a) match (sulphur) ?

٦ـ طبعًا ؛ تفضّل !

6 'ahmad   *Pronounce* : tab$^\epsilon$an ; tafaddal !

  Ahmad   *English* : Of course ; here you are !

٧ـ شكرًا جزيلً . هل تدخّن ؟

7 Jaak   *Pronounce* : shukran jazeelan. Hal tudakhkhin ?

   Jack   *English* : Thank you very much. Do you smoke ?

٨ـ نعم ؛ قليلٌ

8 'ahmad   *Pronounce* : na$^\epsilon$am, qaleelan

    Ahmad   *English* : Yes, a little.

٩ـ كم الساعة ، من فضلك ؟

9 Jaak   *Pronounce* : kami (1) s-saa$^\epsilon$a, min fadlik ?

    Jack   *English* : What time is it (how much the hour) (1), please ?

١٠ـ الثانية و النصف

10 'ahmad   *Pronounce* : 'ath-thaaniya (2) wan-nisf

    Ahmad   *English* : Two thirty (the second (2) and the half).

COMMENTS

1 You are probably puzzled by the word **hal**, which occurs several times in this lesson. This invariable word is used at the beginning of a sentence to make known that what follows is a question. (In spoken Arabic it is not needed, as the tone of voice serves the same purpose.) It changes a statement into a question in the same way as our auxiliary "do" :

    Statement : You work on Sunday.

    Question : **Do** you work on Sunday ?

The closest thing to a translation of **hal** would be : "Is it a fact that... ?"

2 Lessons 3 and 4 contain many examples of typically Arabic **"noun sentences"** — that is, sentences in which there is no connecting verb "to be" between the subject and the predicate. Pay particular attention to this way of saying things, which you will encounter regularly from now on.

In Lesson 3

8 hal 'anta saa'ih, ya sayyidi ?   (Are) you (a) tourist, sir ?

9 la, 'ana fi $^\epsilon$utla   No, I (am) on vacation.

10 'ana $^\epsilon$aa'id 'ila bilaadi   I (am) returning to my country.

16

In Lesson 4

1	hal 'anta tabeeb ?	(Are) you (a) doctor ?
2	la, 'ana mu^εallim ; wa'anta ?	No, I (am a) teacher ; and you ?
3	'ana ṣaḥafi	I (am a) journalist.
9	kami s-saa^εa, min faḍlik ?	What time (is) it, please ?

NOTES

1 The word for "how much" or "how many" is **kam** كَمْ . The word for "the hour" is written **'as-saa^εa** when it is at the beginning of a sentence. But here, because it is not at the beginning of a sentence, the initial **'a** disappears. This leaves us with **kam s-saa^εa** كَمْ الشّاعة . In order to make a smooth connection between the two words, we need a "bridging" vowel. After **kam**, the preferred bridging vowel is the short **i**, which is added to **kam**, making **kami** ; and the phrase thus becomes **kami s-saa^εa** كم الشّاعة . (Notice, however, that in the Arabic script — not in our transcription — the suppressed **'a** remains as a vestigial, unpronounced **'alif.)**

17

In general, when the final consonant of a word has no vowel and the voice has to come to a dead stop on it before it can go on to the following word, a vowel has to be introduced to make the transition. This applies particularly in instances like the present one, in which the following word starts with a "disappearing" 'a. This connecting vowel may be the short i, as in the case of kami (and in most other instances). But the other short vowels are similarly used for such bridges. Here, for example, is a use of a :

min t-taa'ira مِنْ الطَّائِرَة "from the plane" becomes :

mina t-taa'ira مِنَ الطَّائِرَة

2 In reply to the question, "What time is it ?" ("How much the hour ?"), the word for "hour" is often dropped. Instead of the complete reply, "the hour the second", 'as-saa$^\epsilon$a th-thaaniya الشَّاعة الثَّانية , you are likely to hear just "the second", 'ath-thaaniya الثَّانية .

EXERCISES

١ـ كم الشَّاعة، من فضلك ؟

1 kami s-saa$^\epsilon$a, min fadlik ?
What time is it, please ?

٢ـ هل أنت في عطلة الأن ؟

2 hal 'anta fi $^\epsilon$utla l'aan ?
(Are) you on vacation now ?

٣ـ أعطني قهوة بلا حليب

3 'a$^\epsilon$tini qahwa bila haleeb
Give me coffee without milk.

٤ـ نعم ، عندي سجاير

4 na$^\epsilon$am, $^\epsilon$indi sajaayir
Yes, I have cigarettes.

٥ـ لا، لا أُدخّن ؛ شكرًا

5 la, la 'udakh-khin ; shukran

No, I don't smoke ; thankyou.

٦ـ لا أخذ شاي

6 la 'aakudh shaay

I don't drink (take) tea.

Incidental note

The word **shaay** (tea), borrowed from Chinese, is usually invariable. That is, unlike native Arabic words, it rarely has case endings. If it were an Arabic word, it would here have the ending **-an** of an indefinite word in the object case.

الدَّرسُ الخامس

Pronounce
'ad-darsu l-khaamis

English
Fifth Lesson
(The lesson the fifth)

في الطَّائرة

Pronounce : fi t-taa'ira (ti)

English : In the airplane

١ـ هذا العصير لذيد

1 Jaak
Jack

Pronounce : haadha l-ᶜaseer ladheedh
English : This juice (this the juice) (is) delicious.

19

٢ـ ألقهوة أيضًا مضبوطة

2 'aḥmad   *Pronounce* : 'al-qahwa 'aydan maḍbooṭa

Ahmad   *English* : The coffee too (is) perfect.

٣ـ ولكن... أين شنطتي©؟

3 Jaak   *Pronounce* : walaakin .... 'ayna shantati (1) ?

Jack   *English* : (And) but .... where (is) my bag (1) ?

٤ـ هنا، تحت المقعد

4 'aḥmad   *Pronounce* : huna, taḥta l-maq$^\varepsilon$ad

Ahmad   *English* : Here, under the seat (bench).

٥ـ شكرًا . هل تعرف هذه المجلّة؟

5 Jaak   *Pronounce* : shukran. hal ta$^\varepsilon$rif haadhihi l-majalla ?

Jack   *English* : Thankyou. Do you know this magazine (this the magazine) ?

٦ـ طبعًا . هي ممتازة... ولكن ،مابك©؟

6 'aḥmad   *Pronounce* : tab$^\varepsilon$an. Hiya mumtaaza ... walaakin, ma bik (2) ?

Ahmad   *English* : Of course. It (is) excellent, (And) but ... what's wrong (what in you) (2) ?

20

٧- عندي صداع

7 Jaak
Jack

Pronounce : ^εindi sudaa^ε
English : I have a headache.

٨- يا آنستي !

8 'aḥmad
Ahmad

Pronounce : ya 'aanisati !
English : (Oh), Miss !

٩- أعطيني حبّة أسبرين

9 Jaak
Jack

Pronounce : 'a^εteeni habbat 'asbireen
English : Give me an aspirin tablet.

١٠- مع كأس ماء، من فضلِكِ ③

10 Jaak

Jack

Pronounce : ma^εa ka's maa', min fadliki (3)
English : With (a) glass (of) water, please (3).

21

NOTES

1 **Shanta** is the more or less colloquial term for a handbag in general, as opposed to the specific term for a suitcase, **haqeeba**.

2 Notice this specifically Arabic way of saying "What's wrong with you ? " or "What's the matter with you ?" : **ma bik ?** It is similar to the American colloquialism, "What's with you ?" The preposition **bi** most often means "with" but sometimes "in". Don't confuse it with ᶜ**inda** as used in the phrase, **maadha** ᶜ**indak ?** meaning "What is in your possession ?"

3 We have already encountered [Lesson 1, Sentence 2] the plural form of the Arabic term for "please", **min faḍlikum**. This term literally means, "out of your grace". Here we have the term in its feminine singular form (the person addressed being one woman) : **min faḍliki**. The suffixes **-kum** and **-ki** are, as you see, possessive pronouns ("your" in the plural and in the feminine singular) that are attached to the end of the words they modify. Here are a few examples of the use of such possessives :

Newspaper	jareeda(tun)	جريدة
My newspaper	jareedati	جريدتي
Your [masc. sing.] newspaper	jareedatuk(a)	جريدتُكَ
Your [fem. sing.] newspaper	jareedatuki	جريدتُكِ

EXERCISES

١ـ لا أعرف هذه البلاد

1 la 'aᶜrif haadhihi l-bilaad

I do not know (the) country.

[Notice, again, the feminine singular adjective **haadhihi**, with the plural noun, **bilaad**. For the reason why, see page 44.]

٢ـ هل تعرف هذا الطبيب ؟

2 hal taᶜrif haadha t-tabeeb ?

Do you [masc.] know this (the) doctor ?

22

٣ ـ ماذا تعرف في هذا البلد ؟

3 maadha ta‸rif fi haadha l-balad ?
What do you [masc. sing.] know in this (the) country ?

٤ ـ هل تريد كأس ماء ؟

4 hal tureed ka's maa' ?
Do you [masc. sing.] want (a) glass (of) water ?

٥ ـ لا ، أعطني عصير فواكه

5 la, 'a‸tini ‸aseer fawaakih
No, give me (a) fruit juice (juice fruit).

الدّرسُ السّادسى

Pronounce
'ad-darsu s-saadis

English
Sixth Lesson
(The lesson the sixth)

في الطّائِرة

Pronounce : fi t-taa'ira (ti)
English : In the airplane

١ ـ هل نصل قريبًا ؟

1 Jaak   *Pronounce* : hal nasil qareeban ?
   Jack   *English* : Do we arrive soon ?

23

٢- نعم، يا سيّدي : بعد ⓵ خمسِ دقائق

2 'al muḍeefa   *Pronounce* : naᶜam, ya sayyidi, baᶜda (1)
'ila jaak   khamsi daqaa'iq
The stewardess   *English* : Yes, sir, in (after) (1) five
to Jack   minutes.

٣- ألحمدُ لِلَّه ⓶

3 Jaak   *Pronounce* : 'al-hamdu li-llaah (2)
Jack   *English* : That's good news (Praise be to
                 God) (2).

٤- ما ⓷ أسمُك ؟

4 'aḥmad   *Pronounce* : ma (3) smuk ?
Ahmad   *English* : What (3) (is) your name ?

٥- جاك فرنوي ⓸. وأنتَ ؟

5 Jaak   *Pronounce* : Jaak Firnooy (4) ; wa'anta ?
Jack   *English* : Jacques Verneuil (4) ; and yours
                 (you) ?

٦- إسمي : أحمد نبيل

6 'aḥmad   *Pronounce* : 'ismi 'aḥmad Nabeel
Ahmad   *English* : My name (is) Ahmad Nabeel.

٧- تشرّفنا !

7 Jaak   *Pronounce* : tasharrafna
Jack   *English* : I am pleased to meet you (we
                 have been honoured).

٨ـ سيّداتي ، أنِساتي ، سادتي ، قد⁵ وصلنا

8 sawtu
l-mudeefa
Voice of the
stewardess

Pronounce : sayyidaati, 'aanisaati, saadati:
qad (5) waṣalna
English : Ladies, young ladies, gentlemen:
we have (5) arrived.

٩ـ نتمنّى لكم إقامةً طيبةً في بلدنا

9 sawtu
l-mudeefa
Voice of the
stewardess

Pronounce : natamanna lakum 'iqaama-
(tan) ṭayyiba fi bilaadina
English : We wish you [plural] a pleasant
stay in our country.

COMMENT

In Sentence 1, notice how, both in Arabic and in English, the verb
"arrive" contains an implied future. This is a good example of
what we call, in Arabic, a verb in the **"pending aspect"** rather
than in the "present tense" — that is, a verb referring to an
incompleted action. We will have more to say about this later.

NOTES

1 The Arabic expression for **"in** five minutes", meaning "five
minutes from now" is **"after** five minutes" : **ba⁵da** khams daqaa'iq

بعدَ خمس دقائق "Five minutes **ago**" is expressed as "**before** five minutes" : **qabla** khams daqaa'iq قبلَ خمس دقائق

(Numbers will be dealt with in Lesson 15).

2 This everyday phrase, often shortened to "**'al-ḥamdu l-llaah**"
is used for various purposes. As a reply to "How are you ?" it
corresponds roughly to our "Very well, knock on wood". It can
also mean "Fine !" or "What luck !" or "It's about time !" and
so on.

3 As we pointed out in the Notes of Lesson 5, "What ?" is said
in Arabic either by **ma** ما or by **maadha** ماذا.

We have already seen **ma** ما in **ma bik ?** ("What s wrong ?" — literally "What in you ?"). Here we have it in **ma smuk** ("What (is) your name ?"). Examples of **maadha** ماذا are **maadha tureed** ("What do you want ?") and **maadha ^ϵindakum** (" What have you ?").

4 Our traveller is a Frenchman whose name can no more be pronounced in Arabic than in English. The French *-euil* sounds roughly like the *u* of *burn* followed by *ee*. We might therefore transcribe the gentleman's name in English as *Vare-neuil*. But Arabic has no such sound as *-euil* ; and it also has neither the *v* nor the *a* of *Vare*. Mr **Verneuil** therefore has to be re-baptized, in Arabic, **Firnooy**. If his name were Davies or Post, he would be even worse off. (Try it.)

5 The "particle" **qad** قد before a verb in the **completed aspect** serves to emphasize the completion, especially in the immediate past, of the act referred to. It has no meaning in itself except perhaps that of the word "just" in "Mr. Witherspoon has just left the office." The phrase here, **qad wasalna** قد وصلنا might be translated : "We have just arrived." Followed by a verb in the **pending aspect**, **qad** has a function that we will see later.

EXERCISES : Possessives (See p. 28)

١ـ ما أَسمُك ؟

1 ma smuk ?
What (is) your [masc.] name ?

٢ـ إسمي : محمّد

2 'ismi muhammad
My name (is) Muhammad.

26

٣- ما أَسْمُكِ ؟

3 ma smuki ?
What (is) your [fem.] name ?

٤- إِسمي : زينب

4 'ismi Zaynab
My name (is) Zaynab.

٥- ما أَسْمُهُ ؟

5 ma smuhu ?
What (is) his name ?

٦- إِسمُهُ : عمر

6 'ismuhu ᶜumar
His name (is) Omar.

٧- ما أَسْمُها ؟

7 ma smuha ?
What (is) her name ?

٨- إِسمُها : فاطمة

8 'ismuha Faatima
Her name (is) Fatima.

27

GRAMMAR : Some personal subject pronouns and possessives

A. Personal subject pronouns. These are independent words, as in English.

I	'ana	أنـا
You [masc.]	'anta	أنـت
You [fem.]	'anti	أنـتِ
He [or masc. "it"]	huwa	هو
She [or fem. "it"]	hiya	هي
We	naḥnu	نـحـن
You [masc.]	'antum	أنـتـم
They [masc.]	hum	هـم

B. Possessives. These are **attached** to the end of the words they qualify. Their literal meaning is not "my","your", etc., but **of me, of you**, etc.

My name	'ismi	إسمي
Your [sing.] newspaper	jareedatuk	جريدتك
Your [sing. fem.] bag	shantatuki	شنطتك
		حقيبة

28

His coffee	qahwatu**hu**	قهوتُهُ
Her cigarettes	sajaayiru**ha**	سجايرُها
Our country	bilaadu**na**	بلدُنا
Your drinks	mashroobaatu**kum**	مشروباتُكُم
Their teacher	mu^εallimu**hum**	معلّمُهُم

COMMENT

We will mention in passing (and come back to it later) that Arabic personal pronouns have, in addition to singular and plural forms, **dual** forms (for two people or things). For example :

| You two | 'antuma | أنتُما |
| They two | huma | هُما |

Pronounce الدَّرسُ السَّابِع *English*
'ad-darsu s-saabi^ε Seventh Lesson
(The lesson the seventh)

مراجعة

Pronounce : muraaja^εa

English : Revision

We will start this first review lesson with a few simple reminders, then go on to matters that are probably causing you to scratch your head.

1 Pronunciation. Pound away at this ; it will come. The recording will be no end of help. Remember that, in Arabic no less than in English, a consonant or a vowel mispronounced can wholly change the sense of a word. (Think of "**bill**" and "**pill**", of "**gay**" and "**guy**".) If you pronounce **q** as **k**, you will change "heart", **qalb** قلب into "dog", **kalb** كلب .

29

Be especially careful to distinguish between plain and "emphatic" letters (with dots under them) such as ;

t	تريد	You want
ṭ	طائرة	Airplane
d	جريدة	Newspaper
ḍ	من فضلك	Please
s	سيّدي	Gentleman
ṣ	عصير	Juice

2 Arabic script. Our transcriptions indicate all the vowel sounds, whether they are the *letters* used as long vowels or the *signs* over or under consonants that serve as short vowels. These signs are most often omitted from written Arabic ; but we put them in now and then as a help to understanding words that you might not distinguish from other words having the same set of consonants.

3 Noun-sentences. These are sentences in which the verb "to be" (am, are, is), when it has a simple present indicative sense, is omitted between the subject and the predicate. It is omitted because it is merely a neutral connection be-tween them that adds nothing to what they say without it. The term "noun-sentence" is not a very good one (we use it in preference to others that are worse) ; it is the contrary of a "verbal sentence", in which the job of pinning down the relation between subject and predicate (hence the mean-ing of the sentence) is done by a verb. When the verb "to be" does this job — as it does in situations that we will soon encounter — it re-appears.

30

The subject of a noun-sentence must of course be a noun or a pronoun. Its predicate may be almost anything you can think of. Here are some examples of noun-sentences translated into English :

The foreman	(is)	a roughneck.
His wife	(is)	bad-tempered.
She	(is)	from Oklahoma.
Their children	(are)	insolent brats.
Their marriage	(is)	on the rocks.
They	(are)	getting a divorce.
It	(is)	about time.
I	(am)	sorry for them.

We suggest that you keep this unhappy family in mind until noun-sentences become second nature to you.

4 Prepositions. These serve as bolts and screws that hold the parts of a sentence together in a specific way ; without them, a sentence falls apart. The Arabic system of case-endings makes it possible to do without some common prepositions, especially "of" : the case-ending itself *contains* the "of". But when explicit prepositions are used, the words that they govern must always be in the **oblique case**.

We will take a quick look at the prepositions you have already met, with their commonest meanings, and at one or two others that you will soon find useful :

bi and **ma$^\epsilon$a**	with
fi	in
li	for
'ila	to, towards
taḥta	under
ba$^\epsilon$da	after
min	out of (kindness, pity, consideration, etc ; *not* out of one's house or car or wits)
$^\epsilon$inda	at (in the special senses of "at someone's house" or "in someone's possession" ; somewhat like French *chez*, Italian *da*, German *bei*).

31

5 "Have" in Arabic. The English verb "have" means a vast number of things. One can "have" a car, a bank account and a girlfriend. One can also "have", in a very different senses, a cold, a headache, a baby, a drink, a dance, a good time, a fight, a jog around the block. And one can "have" to leave. Arabic has various words for these various meanings. But some of them — especially the ones implying *possession* — are expressed without using a verb at all. The idea is conveyed instead by a combination of the preposition *ᶜinda,* discussed above, with an attached pronoun (me, you, him, her, etc.) As you will need this formula constantly from now on, here it is in full :

Singular

I have	ᶜindi	عندي
You [masc.] have	ᶜindak	عندك
You [fem.] have	ᶜindaki	عندك
He has	ᶜindahu	عنده
She has	ᶜindaha	عندها

Plural

We have	ᶜindana	عندنا
You [masc.] have	ᶜindakum	عندكم
They have	ᶜindahum	عندهم

You will notice that the feminine plural "you" and "they" are omitted, here and elsewhere in this book, as they are not much used in spoken Arabic. But we will mention, for reference, that the feminine "you have" is ᶜinda**kunna** and the feminine "they have" is ᶜinda**hunna**.

32

GRAMMAR : Verbs

After our summary backward glance, we will take a look ahead. In order to move beyond pidgin-Arabic, we need some verbs. We will therefore tackle at once a few of the commonest ones.

Notice, first of all, that the identifying form of the verb is not the infinitive (there is no such animal in Arabic) but the third person singular of its "completed" (usually past) aspect : "he took", "he gave", etc.

Notice, secondly, that we here give you the verbs in their *pending aspect* and in the *indicative mood* (statement of fact). If you are in doubt about the meaning of these terms, refer back to the Introduction, pp. XLVII - XLVIII.

1 TAKE ('akhadha)   (Root : '-KH-DH)

Singular

I take	'aakhudhu	آخُذ
You [masc.] take	ta'khudhu	تأخُذ
You [fem.] take	ta'khudh**eena**	تأخُذِين
He takes	ya'khudhu	يأخُذ
She takes	ta'khudhu	تأخُذ

Plural

We take	na'khudhu	نأخُذ
You take	ta'khudh**oona**	تأخُذون
They take	ya'khudh**oona**	يأخُذون

2 GIVE ('a^ᶜta)   (Root : ^ᶜ-Ṭ-W)

Singular

I give	'u^ᶜṭi	أُعطي
You [masc.] give	tu^ᶜṭi	تعطي
You [fem.] give	tu^ᶜteena	تعطين
He gives	yu^ᶜṭi	يعطي
She gives	tu^ᶜṭi	تعطي

Plural

We give	nu^ᶜṭi	نعطي
You give	tu^ᶜṭoona	تعطون
They give	yu^ᶜṭoona	يعطون

3 KNOW (^ᶜarafa) (in the sense of know **something**)
(Root : ^ᶜ-R-F)

Singular

I know	'a^ᶜrifu	أعرف
You [masc.] know	ta^ᶜrifu	تعرف
You [fem.] know	ta^ᶜrifeena	تعرفين
He knows	ya^ᶜrifu	يعرف
She knows	ta^ᶜrifu	تعرف

34

Plural

We know	na^εrifu	نعرف
You know	ta^εrifoona	تعرفون
They know	ya^εrifoona	يعرفون

4 WANT ('araada)   (Root : R-W-D)

Singular

I want	'ureedu	أُريد
You [masc.] want	tureedu	تريد
You [fem.] want	tureedeena	تريدين
He wants	yureedu	يريد
She wants	tureedu	تريد

Plural

We want	nureedu	نريد
You want	tureed**oona**	تريدون
They want	yureed**oona**	يريدون

COMMENTS

It will be obvious to you, from the verbs that we have just looked at, that the changes in verb forms from person to person follow certain regular models. As these are the standard models for verbs in the pending state (indicative mood), we suggest that you learn them by heart at once.

In the singular

1 The first person (**I**), whether masculine or feminine, always begins with **hamza** (') plus the vowel **a** or **u**, giving **'a** or **'u**. The hamza in question is "stable" — that is, it does not "give way" to the final vowel of the preceding word, as the **'a** of the definite article does.

I take	'aakhudhu	آخُذ
I give	'u$^\epsilon$ti	أُعطي
I know	'a$^\epsilon$rifu	أعرف
I want	'ureedu	أريد

2 The second person (**you**), whether masculine or feminine, always begins with **t**, followed by **a** or **u**, giving **ta** or **tu**.

You take	ta'khudhu	تأخُذ
You give	tu$^\epsilon$ti	تعطي
You know	ta$^\epsilon$rifu	تعرف
You want	tureedu	تريد

2a When the second person (**you**) is feminine, a supplementary ending which identifies it as such is added to the masculine form. This ending is either **-eena** or **-ayna**. (If the final **-a** is not needed to make a vowel-bridge to the word that follows, it is dropped.)

You take	ta'khudheena	تأخُذين
You give	tu$^\epsilon$teena	تعطين
You know	ta$^\epsilon$rifeena	تعرفين
You want	tureedeena	تريدين

36

3 The third person masculine (**he**) always begins with **y**, followed by **a** or **u**, giving **ya** or **yu**.

He takes	ya'khudhu	يَأخُذ
He gives	yu$^\epsilon$ti	يُعطِى
He knows	ya$^\epsilon$rifu	يَعرف
He wants	yureedu	يُرِيد

3a When the third person is feminine (**she** or the feminine **it**), its form is identical with that of the masculine "**you**". For example :

| You [masc.] want | tureedu | تُرِيد |
| She wants | tureedu | تُرِيد |

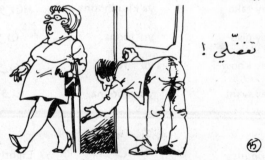

تفضّلي !

In the plural (masculines only)

1 The first person (**we**) begins with **n**, followed by **a** or **u**, giving **na** or **nu**.

We take	na'khudhu	نَأخُذ
We give	nu$^\epsilon$ti	نُعطِى
We know	na$^\epsilon$rifu	نَعرف
We want	nureedu	نُرِيد

37

2 The second person (**you**) begins with **t**, followed by **a** or **u**, giving **ta** or **tu** ; and it ends with **-oona** or **-awna**, which identifies it as the plural form. (The final **a** is again dropped if not needed for "bridging").

You take	ta'khud**hoona**	تأخذون
You give	tu$^\epsilon$**t**oona	تعطون
You know	ta$^\epsilon$rif**oona**	تعرفون
You want	tureed**oona**	تريدون

3 The third person (**they**) begins with **y**, followed by **a** or **u**, giving **ya** or **yu** ; and it ends with the identifying mark of the plural, **-oona** or **-awna**. (The final **a** is again dropped if not needed for "bridging".)

They take	ya'khud**hoona**	يأخذون
They give	yu$^\epsilon$**t**oona	يعطون
They know	ya$^\epsilon$rif**oona**	يعرفون
They want	yureed**oona**	يريدون

الدَّرسُ الثَّامِن

Pronounce
'ad-darsu th-thaamin

English
Eighth lesson
(The lesson the eighth)

فِي المطار

Pronounce : fi l-mataar
English : At the airport

الطَّقسُ مشـمس ـ١

1 'ahmad
Ahmad

Pronounce : 'at-taqs mushmis
English : The weather (is) sunny.

38

٢- في باريس ، كان^٥ الطّقس غائمًا

2	Jaak	*Pronounce* : fi baarees, kaana (1) t-taqs ghaa'im(an)
	Jack	*English* : In Paris, the weather was (1) cloudy.

٣- هيّا[ⓒ] نأخذ[ⓓ] الأمتعة

3	'aḥmad	*Pronounce* : hayya (2) na'khudhi (3) l-'amti^ᶜa
	Ahmad	*English* : Let's (2) get (take) (3) the baggage.

٤- هل عندك بطاقة الشّرطة ؟

4	'aḥmad	*Pronounce* : hal ^ᶜindak bitaaqatu sh-shurṭa ?
	Ahmad	*English* : Have you your landing (police) card ?

٥- لا ، أين هي ؟

5	Jaak	*Pronounce* : la, 'ayna hiya ?
	Jack	*English* : No, where (is) it [fem.] ?

٦- آه ، ها هي ، في جيبي

6	Jaak	*Pronounce* : 'aah ! ha hiya, fi jaybi !
	Jack	*English* : Oh, here it (is), in my pocket !

NOTES

1 Kaana ("was") is the verb "to be" in its **completed aspect**. This calls for some explanations. We have already seen that the verb "to be" normally disappears, in Arabic, when it serves just as a neutral connection between the subject and the predicate of a sentence — that is, when it is in the indicative (or "statement of fact") mood of the pending aspect. "I am a tourist" becomes "I tourist" ; "I am returning" becomes "I returning". However, it re-appears when it is needed for a specific purpose — for example, to make clear that something *will* take place, *may* take place, or *has* taken place.

The pending aspect of "to be", in the indicative mood, is **yakoonu**, meaning "he is". To give it a future sense, we merely add the prefix **sa**. "He will" is thus :

sayakoonu   سيكون

When we want to express the idea that something *may* take place (that we want it to, for example), we use a mood of the verb called the *subjunctive,* which we will look at more closely later on. The expression, "(We want) that he be" is thus.

'an yakoona   أُن يكونَ

Finally, when we want to say that something *has* taken place, we use the **completed aspect** of the verb. "He was" or "he has been" is thus :

kaana   كان

We have said that **kaana** is used when it plays an active role in the sentence ; and, gramatically, it is considered to be an **active verb** in the same way as "throw" or "hit". (The same is true of other Arabic verbs for "not to be" and "become", which we will see later.) Being an active verb, it takes a direct object in the object case (ending in -a when the object is definite, and in **-an** when the object is indefinite). Here are some examples :

The weather **was** cloudy	**kaana** t-taqs ghaa'iman
The weather **will be** sunny	**sayakoonu** t-taqs mushmisan
This juice **was** delicious	**kaana** haadha l-ᶜaseer(u) ladheedhan

Was the trip pleasant ?   hal **kaana** s-safar(u) ṭayyiban ?

2 هَيَّا **hayya** corresponds to the English "let's" in (for example)
"Let's go". It is followed by a verb in the pending aspect. But this
verb serves not to state a fact ("indicative mood") but to express
a semi-command or exhortation ("jussive mood") ; its form is slightly
modified (chopped off at the end) to express this shade of meaning.
For example :

We take [indicative]	na'khudhu	هَيّا نَأخُذ
Let's take [jussive]	hayya na'khudh	
We work [indicative]	na$^\epsilon$malu	هَيّا نَعمَل
Let's work [jussive]	hayya na$^\epsilon$mal	

As you see, what is called the "jussive" corresponds in effect to
what we would call the "imperative" of the first and third persons.
Sometimes we express this as "Let's do something", sometimes by
using "May", as in "May I sink into the ground if that is not true !"
or "May God save the Queen !"

هَيّا نَأخُذ الأَمتِعة !

3 We have just seen, in Note 2, that in the "jussive" mood the
ending of the verb is chopped off. But if the chopped-off verb has
to be linked to a following word by a bridging vowel, the vowel
preferred for this is i. For example :

hayya na'khudh 'al 'amti$^\epsilon$a ("Let's get the baggage") becomes :
hayya na'khudhi l'amti$^\epsilon$a   نَأخُذِ الأَمتِعة

الدَّرسُ التَّاسِع

فى المطار

Pronounce : fi l-mataar

English : At the airport

(A voice reads out what is written on the form :)

١ـ إسم ، لقب ، تأريخ ، ومحلُّ الميلاد

1 sawt   *Pronounce* : 'ism, laqab, ta'reekh wamahallu l-meelaad
      Voice   *English* : Family name, given name, date and place of birth.

٢ـ عنوان ، مهنة ، جنسيّة

2 sawt   *Pronounce* : $^\epsilon$unwaan, mihna, jinsiyya
      Voice   *English* : Address, profession, nationality.

٣ـ رقمُ الجواز ، محلُّ الإقامة

3 sawt   *Pronounce* : raqmu l-jawaaz, mahallu l-'iqaama
      Voice   *English* : Passport number, local address (place of stay).

٤ـ أين الحقائب ؟

4 Jaak   *Pronounce* : 'ayna l-haqaa'ib ?
      Jack   *English* : Where (are) the suitcases [fem.]?

٥ـ تعالَ ! هي قريبة① من هنا

5 'aḥmad   *Pronounce* : taᶜaala ! hiya qareeba (1) min huna

      Ahmad   *English* : Come (along) ! They [fem.] (1) (are) close by (close to here).

٦ـ هيّا نـأخُذها !

6 'aḥmad   *Pronounce* : hayya na'khudh-ha !

      Ahmad   *English* : Let's go and pick them up (take them).

٧ـ أرى حقيبتي : هي هذه الخضراء②

7 Jaak   *Pronounce* : 'ara haqeebati ; hiya, haadhihi l-khadraa' (2)

      Jack   *English* : I see my suitcase ; it (is) this (the) green (one) (2).

٨ـ أَين حقيبتُك ؟

8 Jaak   *Pronounce* : 'ayna haqeebatuk ?

      Jack   *English* : Where (is) your suitcase ?

٩ـ هناكَ ، هي هذه الشَّوداء !

9 'aḥmad   *Pronounce* : hunaaka ; hiya haadhihi s-sawdaa'

      Ahmad   *English* : Over there ; it (is) this (the) black (one).

43

NOTES

1 Here is a special feature of Arabic that you will at first find strange : **the plurals of nouns designating inanimate things** (in this instance, "suitcases") **are dealt with grammatically as if they were feminine singulars.** As a result, the pronoun in this sentence that you would expect to be the plural "they" — meaning "the suitcases" — is in fact the feminine singular "it" **hiya.**

2 As "suitcase" — **haqeeba** — is a feminine noun, its adjective "green", or literally "the green (one)", must also be feminine : **khadraa'.** If the noun here were masculine, "green" in the masculine would be **'akhdar.** In other words, between the masculine and the feminine, the **internal structure** of adjectives of color undergoes a change. Here is a short list of adjectives of color in their masculine and feminine forms, showing these changes :

	Masculine		Feminine	
Black	'aswad	أسود	sawdaa'	سوداء
Green	'akhdar	أخضر	khadraa'	خضراء
Red	'ahmar	أحمر	hamraa'	حمراء
White	'abyad	أبيض	baydaa'	بيضاء
Yellow	'asfar	أصفر	safraa'	صفراء
Blue	'azraq	أزرق	zarqaa'	زرقاء

EXERCICES

١- هل نأخذ حقائبنا ؟

1 hal na'khudh haqaa'ibana ?
Shall we take our suitcases ?

٢- لا ، لا نأخذُها

2 la, la na'khudhuha
No, we won't take them.

44

حقيبتي خضراء ؛ حقيبتك أيضًا ـ٣

3 haqeebati khadraa' ; haqeebatuk 'aydan.
My suitcase (is) green ; your suitcase too.

لا ، حقيبتي سوداء ـ٤

4 la, haqeebati sawdaa'
No, my suitcase (is) black.

هل ترى أمتعتَنا ؟ ـ٥

5 hal tara 'amti$^\epsilon$atana ?
Do you see our baggage ?

نعم ، ولكن ، لا أرى شنطتي ـ٦

6 na$^\epsilon$am, walaakin la 'ara shantati
Yes, but I don't see my (hand) bag.

أين حقيبتك؟ لا أراها ـ٧

7 'ayna haqeebatuk ? la 'araaha
Where (is) your suitcase ? I don't see it.

ما هي جنسيّتك ؟ ـ٨

8 ma hiya jinsiyyatuk ?
What (is) your [sing.] nationality ?

أنا فرنسيّ ـ٩

9 'ana faransi
I (am) French.

ما هذه الحقيبة ؟ ـ١٠

10 ma haadhihi l-haqeeba ?
What (is) this (the) suitcase ?

45

GRAMMAR : Verbs

The **indicative**, in the **pending aspect**, of **SEE (ra'a) (Root : R-'-Y)**
(Remark : We give the English, here and elsewhere, in the form of
the simple present tense : "I see", "you see", etc. But in Arabic,
depending on how the verb is used, it may mean : "I see" or "I am
seeing" or "I will be seeing" — various forms of an act of seeing
that is **not yet completed**.)

Singular

I see	'ara	أَرَى
You [masc.] see	tara	تَرَى
You [fem.] see	tarayna	تَرَيْنَ
He sees	yara	يَرَى
She sees	tara	تَرَى

Plural

We see	nara	نَرَى
You see	tarawna	تَرَوْنَ
They see	yarawna	يَرَوْنَ

46

الدّرسُ العاشر

Pronounce
'ad-darsu l-ᶜaashir

English
Tenth Lesson
(The lesson the tenth)

في المطار

Pronounce : fi l-maṭaar

English : At the airport

١ـ النّاس⁽¹⁾ كثيرون

1 Jaak
Jack

Pronounce : 'an-naas (1) katheeroon
English : There (are) many people (1).
(The people (are) many).

٢ـ كالعادة

2 'aḥmad
Ahmad

Pronounce : kal-ᶜaada
English : As usual (like the habit).

٣ـ أين رجلُ الجمرك ؟

3 Jaak
Jack

Pronounce : 'ayna rajulu l-jumruk ?
English : Where (is) the Customs officer
(the man the Customs) ?

٤ـ ها هو قادم

4 'aḥmad
Ahmad

Pronounce : ha huwa qaadim
English : There he comes (coming).

٥ - ما هي أمتعتك ؟

5 rajulu l-jumruk
ila 'aḥmad

Customs officer
to Ahmad

Pronounce : ma hiya 'amti^εatuk ?

English : What baggage (is) yours ?
(What it [fem.] your baggage) ?

٦ - هذه الحقيبة السّوداء فقط

6 'aḥmad

Ahmad

Pronounce : haadhihi l-ḥaqeeba s-sawdaa'
faqat

English : This black suitcase (this the
suitcase the black) only.

٧ - هل عندك شيء ممنوع ؟

7 rajulu l-jumruk

Customs officer

Pronounce : hal ^εindak shay'
mamnoo^ε ?

English : Have you anything to
declare (forbidden) ?

٨ - تذكار من باريس, لزوجتي
و أولادي

8 'aḥmad

Ahmad

Pronounce : tadh-kaar min baarees, li (2)
zawjati wa'awlaadi

English : A souvenir from Paris, for (2)
my wife and my children.

NOTES

1 In Arabic, as in English, the collective word "people" **'an-naas**
is considered to be a plural, and all words that bear on it (or on
which it has a bearing) must likewise be in the plural. Just as we
say, "The people *are* noisy", Arabic says, "The people (*are*) many" :

'an-naas katheeroon   النّاس كثيرون

48

There is no verb here ; what is in the plural is the adjective "many" or "numerous".

Here are other examples of this. You will notice that the "adjectives" in question are all participles :

The people (are) sitting 'an-naas jaalisoon(a)	النّاس جالسون
The people (are) arriving 'an-naas qaadimoon(a)	النّاس قادمون
The people (are) returning 'an-naas ^ϵaa'idoon(a)	النّاس عائدون

2 **Li** is the Arabic preposition "for" as it is written when it governs a *noun* : "for my *wife*" is **lizawjati**. When it governs a *pronoun*, it changes to **la** : "for *her*" is **laha**. But there is one apparent (rather than real) exception to this. If the pronoun that it governs is "me"— which in Arabic is the letter **yaa'**, pronounced at the end of a word as **i** — then **la** plus **i** is contracted to **li**, "for me".

EXERCISES

١ـ أمتعتي كثيرة

1 'amti^ϵati katheera
I have a lot of baggage (My baggage [fem. sing.] much).

٢ـ هل زوجتك معك ؟

2 hal zawjatuk ma^ϵak ?
(Is) your wife with you ?

٣ـ لا ، هي مع أولادي

3 la, hiya ma^ϵa 'awlaadi
No, she (is) with my children.

٤ـ ما هذا ؟

4 ma haadha ?
What (is) this ?

٥ـ تذكارٌ لأولدِك

5 tadh-kaarun li'awlaadik
A souvenir for your [sing.] children.

49

٦ـ أعطني جوازُك

6 'a $^\epsilon$tini jawaazak
Give [masc.] me your passport.

٧ـ أين زوجتك ؟

7 'ayna zawjatuk ?
Where (is) your wife ?

٨ـ ها هي قادمة

8 ha hiya qaadima
Here she comes (coming).

٩ـ ماذا في حقائبُك ؟

9 maadha fi ḥaqaa'ibik ?
What (is) in your [sing.] suitcases ?

١٠ـ ما عندي شيء ممنوع

10 ma $^\epsilon$indi shay' mamnoo$^\epsilon$
I have nothing to declare (forbidden).

الدَّرسُ الحادي عشر

Pronounce
'ad-darsu l-haadi ᶜashar

في المطار

Pronounce : fi l-mataar

English : At the airport

١- و أُنتَ ، يا سيّدي ،
ما هي أمتعتك ؟

1 rajulu l-jumruk   *Pronounce* : wa'anta, ya sayyidi, ma
                         hiya 'amtiᶜatuk ?

Customs officer   *English* : And you, sir, what baggage
                   (is) yours ?

٢- هذه الشَّنطة و هذه
الحقيبة الخضراء ⓘ

2 Jaak   *Pronounce* : haadhihi sh-shanta wahaa-
              dhihi l-haqeeba l-khadraa' (1)

Jack   *English* : This (the) bag and this green
        (1) suitcase (this the suitcase the
        green).

٣- الجواز ⓒ ، من فضلك

3 rajulu l-jumruk   *Pronounce* : 'al-jawaaz (2), min fadlik
Customs officer   *English* : Passport (2), please.

51

٤- ها هو !

4 Jaak   *Pronounce* : ha huwa
Jack   *English* : Here it (is).

٥- شكرًا ... طيّب ... إفتح هذه الحقيبة !

5 rajulu l-jumruk   *Pronounce* : shukran ...ṭayyib ...'iftaḥ haadhihi l-ḥaqeeba
Customs officer   *English* : Thankyou ... good ... open this suitcase.

٦- و شنطتي أيضًا !

6 Jaak   *Pronounce* : washanṭati 'ayḍan ?
Jack   *English* : And my bag too ?

٧- معلوم !

7 rajulu l-jumruk   *Pronounce* : ma$^\epsilon$loom
Customs officer   *English* : Of course.

٨- بكلّ سرور

8 Jaak   *Pronounce* : bikulli suroor
Jack   *English* : With (all) pleasure.

٩- طيّب ! ما عندك شيء ممنوع

9 rajulu l-jumruk   *Pronounce* : ṭayyib. ma $^\epsilon$indak shay' mamnoo$^\epsilon$
Customs officer   *English* : Good. You have nothing to declare. (You haven't anything forbidden).

١٠ ـ خذ أُمتعتك !

10 rajulu l-jumruk   *Pronounce* : khudh 'amti ^εatak

      Customs officer   *English* : Take your baggage.

١١ ـ شكرًا ، يا سيّدي ـ مع السّلامة !

11 Jaak   *Pronounce* : shukran, ya sayyidi ;
                     ma^εa s-salaama

   Jack   *English* : Thankyou, sir ; good-bye.

١٢ ـ مع السّلامة ⁽³⁾ !

12 rajulu l-jumruk   *Pronounce* : ma^εa s-salaama (3)

      Customs officer   *English* : Good-bye (3).

NOTES

1 For the masculine and feminine forms of colors, see Lesson 9, Note 2.

2 The word used here for "passport" — **jawaaz** — is a shortened version of the complete term جواز سفر **jawaaz safar,** meaning "travel permit".

3 The everyday word for "good-bye", ma^εa s-salaama, actually means "Fare thee well". In principle, therefore, it is a good-bye to someone who is leaving, as is the case here. In fact, it is used in modern Arabic as an all-purpose good-bye.

EXERCISES

١ـ إفتحي هذه الشّنطة !

1 'iftaḥi haadhihi sh-shanṭa
Open [fem.] this bag.

٢ ـ أَعْطِهِ جَوَازَكَ !

2 'a^εtihi jawaazak
Give [masc. sing.] him your passport.

٣ ـ خُذْ حَقِيبَتَها !

3 khudh haqeebataha
Take [masc.] her suitcase.

٤ ـ أَيْنَ أَوْلادُهُم ؟

4 'ayna 'awlaaduhum ?
Where (are) their children ?

٥ ـ ها هُم قادِمون

5 ha hum qaadimoon
Here they come (coming).

إِفْتَحْ هذِهِ الحَقيبَة !

٦ ـ هَلِ الأَمْتِعَةُ مَفْتوحَة ؟

6 hali l-'amti^εa maftooha ?
(Is) the baggage open ?

54

٧- نعم ، ولكن،ما فيها شيء ممنوع

7 na⁶am, walaakin ma feeha shay' mamnoo⁶
Yes, but there is nothing in it to declare (forbidden).

٨ - هل عندهم شيء ممنوع ؟

8 hal ⁶indahum shay' mamnoo⁶ ?
Have they anything to declare (forbidden) ?

٩- هل عندك شهادة تطعيم ؟

9 hal ⁶indak shahaada(t) taṭ⁶eem ?
Have you [sing.] a vaccination certificate ?

١٠ - أين تأشيرتك ؟

10 'ayna ta'sheeratuk ?
Where is your [sing.] visa ?

الدّرسُ الثّاني عشر

Pronounce
'ad-darsu th-thaani ⁶ashar

English
Twelfth Lesson
(The lesson the twelfth)

في المطار

Pronounce : fi l-mataar
English : At the airport

١- أين مكتب تغييرِ النّقود
من فضلك ؟

1 Jaak 'ila
'ahmad
Jack to
Ahmad

Pronounce : 'ayna maktab taghyeeri
n-nuqood min fadlik ?
English : Where (is) the (money)
exchange office, please.

55

٢- هناكَ ، إلى اليمينِ ⓵

2 'ahmad

Ahmad

Pronounce : hunaaka, 'ila l-yameen (1)

English : Over there, to the right (1).

٣- هل تريدُ أن أصحبَك ⓶ ؟

3 'ahmad

Ahmad

Pronounce : hal tureed 'an 'aṣhabak (2) ?

English : Do you want me to (that ١) accompany you (2) ?

٤ - نعم ، تعالَ معي

4 Jaak

Jack

Pronounce : naᶜam, taᶜaala maᶜi

English : Yes, come with me.

٥- ربّما أحتاجُ إلى مساعدتك

5 Jaak

Jack

Pronounce : rubbama 'aḥtaaj 'ila musaaᶜadatik

English : Maybe I will need your help.

٦- أريدُ أن تغيّرَ لي هذه النّقود

6 Jaak 'ila s-sarraaf

Jack to the money-changer

Pronounce : 'ureed 'an tughayyira li haadhihi n-nuqood

English : I'd like you to (I want that you) change this (the) money for me.

56

٧ـ كم معك (3) ؟

7 'as-sarraaf
Money-changer

Pronounce : kam maᶜak (3) ?
English : How much have you (3) ?

٨ـ خمسمائة (4) فرنك فرنسيّ

8 Jaak

Jack

Pronounce : khamsumi'a(ti) farank faransi (4)

English : Five hundred French Francs (4).

٩ـ أعطني النّقود الفرنسيّة حتّى أغيّرها لك

9 'as-sarraaf

Money-changer

Pronounce : 'aᶜtini n-nuqooda l-faransiyya hatta 'ughayyiraha lak

English : Give me the French money to change (so that I may change it) for you.

(الصّرّاف يأخذ النّقود الفرنسيّة ويردّ نقوداً عربيّة)

(*Pronounce* : 'as-sarraaf ya'khudhu n-nuqooda l-faransiyya wayaruddu nuqoodan ᶜarabiyya)

(*English* : The money-changer takes the French money and gives back Arab money.)

١٠ـ تفضّل يا سيّدي... ها هي النّقود العربيّة

10 'as-sarraaf

Money-changer

Pronounce : tafaddal, ya sayyidi...ha hiya n-nuqoodu l-ᶜarabiyya

English : Here you are, sir ; here is the Arab money.

57

NOTES

1 On the right is   ^ϵ**ala** l-yameen   على اليمين

    On the left is   ^ϵ**ala** l-yasaar   على اليسار

    To the right is   '**ila** l-yameen   إلى اليمين

    To the left is   '**ila** l-yasaar   إلى اليسار

2 The subjunctive forms of verbs in the pending aspect are almost the same as the indicative forms. The chief differences are :

(1) all **-u** endings change to **-a** ;

(2) **-eena** changes to **-i** ; and **-ayna** changes to **-ay** ;

(3) **-oona** changes to **-u** plus a "protective" **a** (**alif**) that is written but not pronounced.

Verbs must be in the subjunctive mood when they are in dependent clauses introduced by the conjunction **-an** أَنْ ("that") or **hatta** حَتَّى ("so that", "in order that") or by other conjunctions that we will see later.

3 We have already seen that "have" is most often expressed in Arabic not by a verb but by the preposition ^ϵ**inda** عند meaning "at" or "in my possession", plus an attached pronoun :

I have   = On me (is)   ^ϵ**indi**   عندي

You [sing.] have   = On you (is)   ^ϵ**indak**   عندك

The preposition **ma^ϵa** مع meaning "with", may also be used for this purpose, especially if "have" has the sense of "have on one's person". To illustrate the difference :

Have you [do you possess] any money ?
hal ^ϵ**indak nuqood(un) ?**   هل عندك نقود ؟

Have you any money [on you] ?
hal ma^ϵak nuqood(un) ?   هل معك نقود ؟

The literal meaning of these "noun" sentences is : "(Is there) money in your possession (or on your person) ?" "Money" is the *subject* of the implicit verb, "is", not the *object* of the non-existent verb "have".

4 The word "franc" is in the singular in the Arabic text for reasons that we will explain when we come to the study of Arabic numbers.

58

The number 500, like all other round hundreds, is always followed by a singular noun.

EXERCISES

١- أُريد أنْ تصحبَني

1 'ureed 'an tashabani
I'd like you to (that you) accompany me.

٢- هل تريد أنْ أُغيِّرَ لك هذه النُّقود؟

2 hal tureed 'an 'ughayyira lak haadhihi n-nuqood ?
Do you want me to (that I) change this money for you ?

٣- أعطني نقودًا فرنسيَّة حتّى أُعطيَك نقودًا عربيَّة

3 'a$^\epsilon$tini nuqood(an) faransiyya ḥatta 'u$^\epsilon$tiyak nuqood(an) $^\epsilon$arabiyya
Give me French money so that I may give you Arab money.

٤- إلى كم تحتاج؟

4 'ila kam tahtaaj
How much do you need ? ["Need" = **tahtaaj** plus **'ila.** See p. 65]

٥- هل تحتاج إليَّ؟

5 hal tahtaaj 'ilayya ?
Do you need me ?

ربّما أحتاج الى مساعدتك

59

GRAMMAR : Verbs

The **subjunctive**, in the **pending aspect**, of ACCOMPANY (sahiba)

(Root : S-H-B)

Singular

That I accompany	'an 'ashaba	أن أصحَبَ
That you [masc.] accompany	'an tashaba	أن تصحَبَ
That you [fem.] accompany	'an tashabi	أن تصحبي
That he accompany	'an yashaba	أن يصحَبَ
That she accompany	'an tashaba	أن تصحَبَ

Plural

That we accompany	'an nashaba	أن نصحَبَ
That you accompany	'an tashabu	أن تصحَبوا
That they accompany	'an yashabu	أن يصحَبوا

الدَّرسُ الثَّالثَ عشرَ

English
Thirteenth lesson
(The lesson the thirteenth)

Pronounce
'ad-darsu th-thaalith ^eashar

في المطار

Pronounce : fi l-mataar
English : At the airport

١ـ أيـنَ بابُ الخروج ؟

1 Jaak	*Pronounce* : 'ayna baabu l-khurooj ?
Jack	*English* : Where (is) the exit door ?

60

٢- مِنْ هُنا، إلى اليَسار، في نِهايةِ
المَمَرِّ

| 2 'aḥmad | *Pronounce* : min huna, 'ila l-yasaar, fi nihaayati l-mamarr |
| Ahmad | *English* : From here, to the left, at the end of the corridor. |

٣- هَلْ هُناكَ⓪ مَوْقِف تاكسي،
قَريبًا مِنْ هُنا ؟

| 3 Jaak | *Pronounce* : hal hunaaka (1) mawqif taksi qareeban min huna ? |
| Jack | *English* : Is there (1) a taxi station near (from) here ? |

٤- عِنْدي سَيّارة . سَأُصحِبُكَ؛ إلى
أَيْنَ تَذْهَبُ ؟

| 4 'aḥmad | *Pronounce* : ᶜindi sayyaara, sa'aṣḥabuk. 'ila 'ayna tadhhab ? |
| Ahmad | *English* : I have a car. I will accompany you. Where are you going ? |

٥- إلى فُنْدُق السَّلام

| 5 Jaak | *Pronounce* : 'ila funduqi s-salaam |
| Jack | *English* : To the Peace Hotel. |

٦- أَعْرِفُه؛ هذا فُنْدُق كَبير !

| 6 'aḥmad | *Pronounce* : 'aᶜrifuhu ; haadha funduq kabeer ! |
| Ahmad | *English* : I know it ; it (this) is a large hotel. |

٧- ولكن، لا أريد أن أُزْعِجَك ⑦

7 Jaak

Pronounce : walaakin la 'ureed 'an 'uz^{ε}ijak (2)

Jack

English : But I don't want to (that I) bother you (2).

٨- أبداً؛ يسرُّني أن أصحبَك ⑧

8 'aḥmad

Pronounce : 'abadan ; yasurruni 'an 'aṣhabak (3)

Ahmad

English : Not at all ; I would be glad (it gives me pleasure) to (that I) accompany you (3).

٩- هل هذا الفندق بعيد عن هنا ؟

9 Jaak

Pronounce : hal haadha l-funduq ba^{ε}eed ^{ε}an huna ?

Jack

English : (Is) this hotel far from here ?

١٠- لا، هو قريب

10 'aḥmad

Pronounce : la, huwa qareeb

Ahmad

English : No, it (is) nearby.

١١- سنصل إليهِ بعدَ ربعِ ساعةٍ فقط ⑪

11 'aḥmad

Pronounce : sanaṣil 'ilayhi ba^{ε}da rub^{ε}i saa^{ε}a faqat (4)

Ahmad

English : We will be there (arrive at it) in no more than a quarter of an hour (after a quarter hour only) (4).

62

NOTES

1 This is one way of saying "there is" or "there are" in Arabic. It corresponds exactly to the English expression, being simply "there", **hunaaka** هُنَاكَ plus "is" or "are" (which in Arabic is implied but not written). The question "Is there a hotel ?" is thus written :

hal hunaaka funduq ?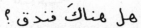

هل هناك فندق ؟

Another way of saying "there is" in Arabic is to use the term "it exists", **yoojad** يوجد . The statement then becomes, "Exists a hotel" (in Arabic sentences, the verb usually precedes the subject) ; and the question, with the interrogative **hal**, becomes "Does (there) exist a hotel ?"

hal yoojad funduq ?

هل يوجد فندق ؟

The verb **yoojad** is generally used in its masculine form even when the thing that exists is feminine.

2 and 3 Notice the -a endings in the subjunctive forms of the verbs **uz^εijak** (bother you) and **'ashabak** (accompany you). The subjunctive forms are required by "I don't want that..." and "It would give me pleasure that..." [See page 58, Note 2]

4 The word for "quarter" (a fourth), **rub^ε**, has the same root as the word for "four", **'arba^εa..**

EXERCISES

ا ـ لا نريد أن يزعجنا

1 la nureed 'an yuz^εijana
We do not want him to (that he) bother us.

٢ ـ يسرّنا أن نصحبكم

2 yasurruna 'an nashabakum
We are glad to accompany you [plur.] (It gives us pleasure that we accompany you).

٣ ـ هل تعرف إلى أين يذهب ؟

3 hal ta^εrif 'ila 'ayna yadhhab ?
Do you know (to) where he is going ?

٤ـ رُبّما أزعجكم ؟

4 rubbama 'uz^εijukum ?
  Perhaps I am bothering you [plur.] ?

٥ـ سأذهب بعد ربعِ ساعةٍ

5 sa'adhhab ba^εda rub^εi saa^εa
  I shall go in (after) a quarter (of an) hour.

GRAMMAR : Verbs
The **indicative (singular** only), in the **pending aspect,** of a few
more common verbs.

CHANGE (ghayyara) (in the sense of ''alter'' or ''modify'')
                (Root : GH-Y-R)

I change [something]	'ughayyir(u)	أُغيِّر
You [masc.] change	tughayyir(u)	تُغيِّر
You [fem.] change	tughayyireen(a)	تُغيِّرين
He changes	yughayyir(u)	يُغيِّر
She changes	tughayyir(u)	تُغيِّر

أين باب
الخروج ؟

GO (dhahaba)　　　　(Root : DH-H-B)

I go	'adhhab(u)	أَذهب
You [masc.] go	tadhhab(u)	تذهب
You [fem.] go	tadhhabeen(a)	تذهبين
He goes	yadhhab(u)	يذهب
She goes	tadhhab(u)	نذهب

But the act of going is more usually expressed by a "noun-phrase" made up of the personal subject pronoun plus the active participle (-ing) of the verb, which is declined like a noun or an adjective :

I (am) going	'ana dhaahib	أنا ذاهب
You [masc.] (are) going	'anta dhaahib	أنت ذاهب
You [fem.] (are) going	'anti dhaahiba	أنتِ ذاهبة
He (is) going	huwa dhaahib	هو ذاهب
She (is) going	hiya dhaahiba	هي ذاهبة

NEED ('ihtaaja plus the preposition 'ila, "to") (Root : H-W-J)

I need	'ahtaaj 'ila	أحتاج إلى
You [masc.] need	tahtaaj 'ila	تحتاج ،،
You [fem.] need	tahtaajeen 'ila	تحتاجين ،،
He needs	yahtaaj 'ila	يحتاج ،،
She needs	tahtaaj 'ila	تحتاج ،،

Pronounce : muraaja⁽ᵉ⁾a مراجـعـة
English : Review

In this lesson we will review a certain number of points raised in the preceding lessons and anticipate questions that you probably have on them ; we will also break a little new ground.

1 The verb kaana, "he was". We saw in Lesson 8 that the verb "to be", though it disappears as a present indicative in normal sentences such as "I (am) a scoundrel", or "You (are) bothering me", where it is just a neutral connection between subject and predicate, reappears when it is needed for a specific purpose. It is most common in its **completed aspect,** which makes clear that the situation referred to has already taken place. In its **pending aspect,** the indicative mood is used chiefly to situate something in the future ; and the subjunctive is used for the purposes mentioned above in connection with the subjunctives of all verbs. At the end of this lesson, you will see how this verb is conjugated in its completed and its pending aspects.

Remember that **kaana** is an active (or "transitive") verb in Arabic, and that it accordingly takes a direct object in the object case. "He was happy" is written : kaana masrooran. "The office will be open" is written : sayakoonu l-maktab maftoohan.

The same principle applies also to other verbs of the same sort which we will meet later, such as "not to be", "become" and "remain".

2 Plurals of nouns designating inanimate things. Remember that these are always dealt with grammatically as **feminine singulars** [See Lesson 9, Note 1]. For example :

The office [singular] is open until one o'clock : **'al maktab maftooh hatta l-waahida** [Masculine singular noun and adjective].

Are the offices [plural] open until the evening ? : **hal(i) l-makaatib maftooha hatta l-masaa'** ? [Masculine plural noun, feminine singular adjective].

66

3 Feminine singulars of nouns and adjectives. As we pointed out in the Introduction, Arabic nouns are of either masculine or feminine gender. But many nouns (as well as adjectives and participles assimilated to nouns) may have both masculine and feminine forms. For example, a tourist or a journalist may be a man or a woman, and so on. In the singular, the commonest way to make a feminine from a masculine is to add to the basic masculine word (that is, to the word *without its case ending* : to **kaatib**, not to **kaati-bun**) the feminine ending -**at**. This ending consists of the short vowel **a** plus a **t** written in a special way (like a dotted h), which is called a **taa' marboota** ﺔ or ة [See Introduction, p. XVII]. The **taa' marboota**, though always *written* when the context requires it, is *pronounced* only when it is followed by a case ending or a suffix that is likewise pronounced. For example, the word for a lady tourist is **saa'iha** ; but if it is pronounced with its case ending, it becomes saa'ih**atun** (subject), saa'ih**atan** (object), or saa'ih**atin** (oblique).

Here are some examples of masculine/feminine words :

Tourist	Masc.	saa'ih	سائح
	Fem.	saa'iha	سائحة
Coming	Masc.	qaadim	قادم
	Fem.	qaadima	قادمة
Journalist	Masc.	ṣaḥafi	صحفي
	Fem.	ṣaḥafiyya	صحفية
Pleasant	Masc.	ṭayyib	طيّب
	Fem.	ṭayyiba	طيّبة
Excellent	Masc.	mumtaaz	ممتاز
	Fem.	mumtaaza	ممتازة

4 The use of active participles as adjectives. In English, the sentence, "The man is working" is made up of a subject, "the man", and of a verb in the "continuous present" tense, "is working". This is in turn made up of the auxiliary, "is", plus the participle, "working". In Arabic, this kind of participle is considered to be (and to function) not as part of a verb but as an **adjective**, in the same way as "rich" or "angry" or "pink". The sentence, "The man is working" is thus a "noun sentence" in which the subject is "the man", the predicate is the adjective "working", and the verb "is" disappears. We have already seen that the phrase, "Here she comes" is written, in Arabic, "Here she (is) coming", **ha hiya qaadima.** Similarly, "He (is) returning to the office", **huwa ᶜaa'id 'ila l-maktab,** is a noun sentence whose subject is "he" and whose predicate is "returning".

5 Subjunctives. A verb is put in the "subjunctive mood" when it designates an action that is subordinate to (or dependent on) a wish, an intention, a purpose or a sentiment (hoping, fearing, etc.), expressed in a verb that precedes it. For example, in the sentence, "I hope that we meet soon", the verb "meet" is subordinate to the act of hoping. Subordinate clauses containing verbs in the subjunctive mood are always introduced by the conjunction "that".

We have already seen (in Lesson 12, Note 2) how the subjunctives of verbs are formed. Now we will look at a few kinds of "that" which require the subjunctive after them.

(a) The simple "that" : 'an أَنْ , as in "I want that...",

'ureed 'an أُرِيـد أَن or "I wish that", 'arju 'an

أَرْجو أَن , or "I am happy that" [literally, "It rejoices

me that"], yasurruni 'an يَسُرّني أَن . Here are some
examples :

I want you to (that you) open the door : **'ureed 'an taftaha l-baab**
We wish that your stay be pleasant (We wish you a pleasant stay) : **narju 'an takoona 'iqaamatukum tayyiba**

68

It rejoices me to (that I) see you : **yasurruni 'an 'araak**

I am glad to (it rejoices me that I) accompany you to the hotel : **yasurruni 'an ashabak 'ila l-funduq**

(b) "So that" : **hatta** حَتَّى . For example :
Come with me so as to (so that we may) take the suitcases :

ta$^\epsilon$aala ma$^\epsilon$i hatta na'khudha l haqaa'ib

(c) "In order that" : **li** لِ or **likay** لِكَيْ

GRAMMAR : Verbs

The verb **kaana**, "he was", in various forms (**Root : K-W-N**)

Completed aspect

I was (or have been)	kuntu	كُنْت
You [masc.] were (or have been)	kunta	كُنْت
You [fem.] were (or have been)	kunti	كُنْت
He was (or has been)	kaana	كَانَ
She was (or has been)	kaanat	كَانَتْ

Pending aspect, indicative mood

I am (or will be)	'akoonu	أَكُون
You [masc.] are (or will be)	takoonu	تَكُون
You [fem.] are (or will be)	takooneena	تَكُونِين
He is (or will be)	yakoonu	يَكُون
She is (or will be)	takoonu	تَكُون

Pending aspect, subjunctive mood

That I be	'an 'akoona	أَن أَكُونَ
That you [masc.] be	'an takoona	أَن تَكُونَ
That you [fem.] be	'an takooni	أَن تَكُونِي
That he be	'an yakoona	أَن يَكُونَ
That she be	'an takoona	أَن تَكُونَ

GRAMMAR : Yoked couples

Two oxen hitched to the same plow are generally yoked together. In popular mythology, two people held together by the yoke of marriage walk the same path. In Arabic grammar, when two words form a unit held together by "of" — which is expressed not by a corresponding preposition (there is no "of" in Arabic) but by the **oblique case ending** on the word governed by "of" — they similarly form a "yoked couple". Here are some examples of such yoked couples in English. You will notice that, in all of them, one or another kind of "of" is either expressed or implied.

Fruit juice	The sheikh's Cadillac
City hall	Abdul's son
Passport application	The emperor's new clothes
Vaccination certificate	A pack of cigarettes
Exit visa	A handful of dust
Groucho's moustache	The end of the day
Marilyn's smile	The problems of the world

In Arabic, when words are yoked in this way, **the word governed by "of" automatically makes the preceding word definite,** even though it may be preceded by an implied "a". Thus, when Jack says to the stewardess [Lesson 2, Sentence 8], "Give me (a) pack of cigarettes" — 'a$^\epsilon$teeni $^\epsilon$ulbata sajaayir — the word for "pack", $^\epsilon$ulbata, has the object-case ending for **definite** words, -a, not the indefinite -an ending that you would expect.

From now on, you will meet constantly such yoked couples, so you would do well to grasp at once the principle

70

behind their behaving as they do. (You can safely forget that the grammatical term for yoked couples is "words in the construct state".)

COMMENTS

Starting with the next lesson, we will change the layout of the pages so as to make room for longer sentences. The Arabic text will be printed on the left-hand page, the pronunciation and the English facing it on the right. This will allow you to practise reading complete pages of Arabic script without referring to the transcribed and translated text unless you need to.

إلى الفندق

(أحمد يفتحُ لجاك بابَ السَّيّارة)

١ـ تفضَّلْ !

(جاك يدخل و يجلس)

٢ـ شُكرًا ؛ سيّارتُك مريحة
و واسعــة

٣ـ نعم ، هي مناسبة ِللأُولاد

٤ـ كمْ[0] ولدًا عندك ؟

٥ـ عندي أربعةُ أولاد

The lesson the fifteenth

Pronounce : 'ila l-funduq
English : To the hotel

(*Pronounce* : 'aḥmad yaftaḥ lijaak baaba s-sayyaara)
(*English* : Ahmad opens the car door for Jack)

1 'aḥmad — *Pronounce* : tafaḍḍal
Ahmad — *English* : After you. [See note on tafaḍḍal, p. 7]

(*Pronounce* : jaak yadkhul wayajlis)
(*English* : Jack gets in and sits down.)

2 Jaak — *Pronounce* : shukran ; sayyaaratuk mureeḥa wawaasi$^{\epsilon}$a
Jack — *English* : Thankyou ; your car (is) comfortable and roomy.

3 'aḥmad — *Pronounce* : na$^{\epsilon}$am, hiya munaasiba lil'awlaad
Ahmad — *English* : Yes, it is practical for the children.

4 Jaak — *Pronounce* : kam (1) walad(an) $^{\epsilon}$indak ?
Jack — *English* : How many (1) children have you ?

5 'aḥmad — *Pronounce* : $^{\epsilon}$indi 'arba$^{\epsilon}$a(tu) 'awlaad
Ahmad — *English* : I have four children.

$$٦ - ثلاثة ⑤ صبيان ⑥ وبنت واحدة$$

$$٧ - هل أنت متزوِّج ؟$$

$$٨ - لا، أنا أعزب$$

NOTES

1 There are two ways of saying "how much ?" or "how many ?" in Arabic.

(a) The simplest and commonest way is to use the word **kam** كم followed directly by the noun for the persons or things in question, always in the **singular**, whatever the number of persons or things, and in the **object/adverb case**.

(b) Another (less common) way is to use **kam** plus the preposition **min** مِن , followed again by a singular noun but in the **oblique case**. This combination of words, which can be split (**kam...min**), means, in effect : How much (or how many) *in the way of* or *by way of* or *in terms of...* ?

Here are examples of both expressions :

How many suitcases have you ?
(a) **kam** ḥaqeeba(tan) $^\epsilon$indak ?   كم حقيبة عندك ؟
or
(b) **kam** $^\epsilon$indak **min** ḥaqeeba(tin)

How many children have you ?
(a) **kam** walad(an) $^\epsilon$indak ?   كم ولدًا عندك ؟
or
(b) **kam** $^\epsilon$indak **min** walad(in) ?

How many cigarettes have you ?
(a) **kam** seejaara(tan) ma$^\epsilon$ak ?   كم سيجارة معك ؟
or
(b) **kam** ma$^\epsilon$ak **min** seejaara(tin) ?

74

6 'ahmad   *Pronounce* : thalaatha(tu) sibyaan (2)
                            wabint(un) (3) waahida

      Ahmad   *English* : Three boys (2) and one girl (3).

7 'ahmad   *Pronounce* : hal 'anta mutazawwij ?
      Ahmad   *English* : Are you married ?

8 Jaak   *Pronounce* : la, 'ana 'a$^\epsilon$zab
      Jack   *English* : No, I (am a) bachelor.

2 This is the plural of the word for "young boy" or "lad" :

sabiyyun صِبْيَةٌ

3 The word **bint** بنت means "girl" in general, but is also commonly used to mean "daughter", as in "my daughter" :
binti. The more correct way of saying "daughter" is to put the word for "son", **'ibn(un)** إبن into the feminine :
'ibna(tun). Hence :

My son   =   **'ibni**   إبْني

My daughter =   **'ibnati**   إبْنَتي

The initial hamza with its vowel, -i, disappears when either of these words is preceded by another word. It is replaced by the vowel of the preceding word (for example, **'ibnati wabni** = my daughter and my son) or else by an appropriate bridging-vowel.

The same is true of the word **'ism**, "name". For example, "What (is) your name ?" is written : **masmuk ?** (Answer : **'ismi muhammad**, "My name (is) Muhammad".)

GRAMMAR : Cardinal Numbers from 1 to 10

If you like puzzles and games, Arabic numbers will amuse you ; if not, a little playfulness of mind will help. The rules of this game are a bit complicated ; but we will try to present them as simply as we can and in small packages, starting in this lesson with the numbers from 1 to 10, which you will find tabulated on page 77.

Just one preliminary remark, which we hope will not frighten you off : Except for 1 and 2, which behave like adjectives, **all Arabic numbers are nouns** (*a* so-many *of* something or *with respect to* something). Some of these number-nouns (the ones from 3 to 9) change gender, like oysters, with the circumstances, as we shall see below. Others (20, 30, 40... 90) are masculine plurals by nature and remain so in all circumstances. The round hundreds are always feminine ; and, with one exception, they are singular as they are in English ("five *hundred* sheep"). (The exception is 200, which is "dual".) The word for 1000 is a masculine singular and remains so ; the other thousands are plurals (except for 2000, which is again a "dual"). This much said, we will look at the individual numbers.

1 One is fairly clear sailing. It is written **waahid** in the masculine and **waahida** in the feminine. It is an adjective that *follows* its noun and *agrees* with it in gender :

One child [masc.]   **walad(un) waahid**   ولدٌ واحدٌ

One girl [fem.]   **bint(un) waahida**   بنتٌ واحدة

2 Two is **'ithnaan(i)** [masc.]   إتنَان   or **'ithnataan(i)**

[fem.]   إتنتَان   . It is likewise an adjective that *follows* its

noun and *agrees* with it in gender :

Two children [masc.]   **waladaani thnaan(i)**

Two cars [fem.]   **sayyaarataani thnataan(i)**

However, the word "two" is more or less superfluous in Arabic except when it is needed for emphasis, as in : "We had *two* beers, not three." The idea of two-ness is expressed by the "dual" ending of the noun itself, which you have just seen on both the noun and

its number : -aan(i)   أَن   . To express unemphatically "two

children" or "two cars", it is enough to say :

waladaan(i)   ولدَان

sayyaarataan(i)   سيّارتَان

3 - 10 It is with **"three"** — **thalaath(un)** [masc. form] and **thalaatha(tun)** [fem. form] — that the numbers become tricky. "Seven books" becomes in Arabic *"a seven of books"*. The "of" is expressed by the oblique case ending on "books". And "books" is in the plural. You will say, "Of course !" But you will soon see that the numbers from 3 to 10 are the *only* ones that take plurals after them. So far, so good. But now watch closely : If the thing counted is masculine, the number is feminine, and vice-versa. That is, **the gender of these numbers agrees upside-down with the gender of what is counted.** Here are a couple of examples of this perverse behavior.

A. We want to say "five offices" :

"Office" is a *masculine* noun

maktab   مكتب

76

Its plural is
    makaatib مكاتب

The *feminine* form of "five" is
    khamsa(tun) خمسة

"(A) five (of) offices" is therefore
    khamsa(tu) makaatib خمسةُ مكاتب

B. We want to say "three ladies" :

"Lady" is a *feminine* noun
    sayyida سيّدة

Its plural is
    sayyidaat(un) سيّدات

The *masculine* form of "three" is
    thalaath(un) ثلاث

"(A) three (of) ladies" is therefore
    thalaath(u) sayyidaat(in) ثلاثُ سيّدات

Here is a table of the Arabic cardinal numbers from 1 to 10.

(Note that, when *counting* from 1 to 10, you should use the forms in the left-hand column.)

	With a masculine noun		With a feminine noun	
1 (١)	waaḥid	واحد	waaḥida(tun)	واحدة
2 (٢)	'ithnaan(i)	إثنان	'ithnataan(i)	إثنتان
3 (٣)	thalaatha(tun)	ثلاثة	thalaath(un)	ثلاث
4 (٤)	'arba$^\epsilon$a(tun)	أربعة	'arba$^\epsilon$(un)	أربع
5 (٥)	khamsa(tun)	خمسة	khams(un)	خمس
6 (٦)	sitta(tun)	ستة	sitt(un)	ست
7 (٧)	sab$^\epsilon$a(tun)	سبعة	sab$^\epsilon$(un)	سبع
8 (٨)	thamaaniya(tun)	ثمانية	thamaanin	ثمان
9 (٩)	tis$^\epsilon$a(tun)	تسعة	tis$^\epsilon$(un)	تسع
10 (١٠)	$^\epsilon$ashra(tun)	عشرة	$^\epsilon$ashr(un)	عشر

77

إلى الفندق

١- تتكلّمُ العربيّة جيّدًا

٢- شكرًا ... أفهم جيّدًا

٣- ولكن، أتكلّم بِصعوبة

٤- أين تعلّمتَ العربيّة ؟

٥- في باريس

٦- حسنًا جدًّا ! ... ها هي
المدينة ... ألفندق أمامَنا .

The lesson the sixteenth

Pronounce : 'ila l-funduq
English : To the hotel

1 'ahmad

Ahmad

Pronounce : tatakallamu l-ᶜarabiyya jayyidan
English : You speak Arabic well.

2 Jaak

Jack

Pronounce : shukran ... 'afham jayyidan
English : Thank you ... I understand (it) well.

3 Jaak

Jack

Pronounce : walaakin 'atakallam bisuᶜooba
English : But I speak (it) with difficulty.

4 'ahmad

Ahmad

Pronounce : 'ayna taᶜallamta l-ᶜarabiyya?
English : Where did you learn Arabic ?

5 Jaak

Jack

Pronounce : fi baarees
English : In Paris.

6 'ahmad

Ahmad

Pronounce : hasan(an) jiddan ! Ha hiya l-madeena ... 'al-funduq 'amaamana
English : Bravo ! Here we are in town (Here it [fem.] (is) the town)... The hotel (is) in front of us.

79

٧ـ فعلاً ! هذا الفندق
كبيرٌ جدّاً

(يصلانِ أمامَ بابِ الفندق)

٨ـ والآنَ ، سآخذ أمتعتك !

٩ـ لا ، أنا آخذُها [1]

١٠ـ إذن ، خذِ الشَّنطة ، وأنا
آخذُ الحقيبة الكبيرة

خذ الحقيبة
وأنا آخذ الشَّنطة

7 Jaak   *Pronounce* : fi€lan ! haadha l-funduq kabeerun jiddan

    Jack   *English* : So it is ! It's a very large hotel (This hotel is very large).

(*Pronounce* : yaṣilaani 'amaama baabi l-funduq
(*English* : They arrive in front of the hotel door.)

8 'aḥmad   *Pronounce* : wal'aan, sa'aakhudh 'amti€atak !

    Ahmad   *English* : And now, I'll take your baggage.

9 Jaak   *Pronounce* : la, 'ana 'aakhudhuha (1)

    Jack   *English* : No, I'll take it (1).

10 'aḥmad   *Pronounce* : 'idhan, khudhi sh-shanta, wa'ana 'aakhudhu l-haqeeba l-kabeera

    Ahmad   *English* : In that case, take the bag and I'll take the big suitcase.

NOTES

1 As we pointed out on page 3 (Note 1), a verb in the pending aspect (which may refer to a present or a future time) is given a specifically future sense by placing before it the particle **sa** or

sawfa : سَ ـ سَوْفَ

But when, as in this case, the action referred to is in the immediate future, or when the future sense is clear from the context, the particle is often dropped. Here we have both forms :

Sentence 8 :   I'll take your baggage   سَأخذ أُمتعتك
              sa'aakhudh'amti€atak

Sentence 9 :   No, I'll take it   لا ، أَنا أَخذُها
              la, 'ana **'aakhudh**uha

EXERCISES

١- هل تفهمُ العربيّة جيّدًا ؟

1 hal tafhamu l-ᶜarabiyya jayyidan ?
Do you understand Arabic well ?

٢- أفهمُ العربيّة و لكن، أتكلّمُها بصعوبة

2 'afhamu l-ᶜarabiyya, walaakin, 'atakallamuha biṣuᶜooba
I understand Arabic, but I speak it with difficulty.

٣- تتكلّمُ الفرنسيّة جيّدًا ؟
أين تعلّمتـها ؟

3 tatakallamu l-faransiyya jayyidan ; 'ayna taᶜallamtaha ?
You speak French well ; where did you learn it ?

٤- هنا، في هذه المدينة الكبيرة

4 huna, fi haadhihi l-madeena l-kabeera
Here, in this big city.

٥- يتكلّمُ الفرنسيّة بصعوبة،
و لكن، يفهمُ جيّدًا

5 yatakallamu l-faransiyya biṣuᶜooba, walaakin yafham(u)
jayyidan
He speaks French with difficulty, but he understands
(it) very well.

GRAMMAR : Verbs

Here are the **singulars** of some more common verbs, in the **indicative** mood. We give the first two in their **pending aspect**, the third in its **completed aspect**.

Pending aspect of SPEAK (takallama) (Root : K-L-M)

I speak	'atakallamu	أتكلّم
You [masc.] speak	tatakallamu	تتكلّم
You [fem.] speak	tatakallameena	تتكلّمين
He speaks	yatakallamu	يتكلّم
She speaks	tatakallamu	تتكلّم

Pending aspect of UNDERSTAND (fahima) (Root : F-H-M)

I understand	'afhamu	أفهم
You [masc.] understand	tafhamu	تفهم
You [fem.] understand	tafhameena	تفهمين
He understands	yafhamu	يفهم
She understands	tafhamu	تفهم

Completed aspect of LEARN (ta$^\epsilon$allam) (Root : $^\epsilon$-L-M)

I learned	ta$^\epsilon$allamtu	تعلّمت
You [masc.] learned	ta$^\epsilon$allamta	تعلّمت
You [fem.] learned	ta$^\epsilon$allamti	تعلّمت
He learned	ta$^\epsilon$allama	تعلّم
She learned	ta$^\epsilon$allamat	تعلّمت

في الفندق

(جاك و أحمد يدخلانِ الفندق)

١- تفضّل !

٢- شكرًا

(يستقبلُهما صاحبُ الفندق)

٣- مرحبًا[5]!

٤- هل عندكم غرفة لهذا السّيّد ؟

٥- نعم، يا سيّدي ... وأنت، هل
تريد غرفة أيضًا ؟

The lesson the seventeenth

Pronounce : fi l-funduq
English : At (in) the hotel

(*Pronounce* : jaak wa'aḥmad yadkhulaani l-funduq
(*English* : Jack and Ahmad enter the hotel.)

1 'aḥmad	*Pronounce* : tafaḍḍal	
Ahmad	*English* : After you.	

2 Jaak	*Pronounce* : shukran	
Jack	*English* : Thank you.	

(*Pronounce* : yastaqbiluhuma ṣaaḥibu l-funduq)
(*English* : The hotel manager receives them.)

3 saaḥibu l-funduq	*Pronounce* : marḥaban ! (1)	
Hotel Manager	*English* : Welcome ! (1)	

4 'aḥmad	*Pronounce* : hal ᶜindakum ghurfa lihaadha s-sayyid ?	
Ahmad	*English* : Have you a room for this gentleman ?	

5 saaḥibu l-funduq	*Pronounce* : naᶜam, ya sayyidi ... wa'anta; hal tureed ghurfa 'aydan ?	
Hotel Manager	*English* : Yes, sir ... And (what about) you ; do you want a room also ?	

٦ـ لا، هذه الغرفة لي وحدي (٥)

٧ـ هذا السّيّد يصحبني فقط

٨ـ طيّب... هذا (٣) هو مفتاحُ
غرفتك

٩ـ الرّقم : ثلاثون (٤)، في
الطّابقِ الثّالث

١٠ـ هل معك أمتعة ؟

١١ـ نعم : هذه الشّنطة و هذه
الحقيبة الكبيرة

6 Jaak   *Pronounce* : la, haadhihi l-ghurfa li waḥdi (2)

    Jack   *English* : No, only I need a room (this room is for me only (2).

7 Jaak   *Pronounce* : haadha s-sayyid yaṣḥabuni faqat

    Jack   *English* : This gentleman is just accompanying me [faqaṭ = "just"].

8 ṣaaḥibu   *Pronounce* : ṭayyib ... haadha (3) huwa
l-funduq   miftaaḥ(u) ghurfatik

    Hotel   *English* : Fine ... here is (3) the key of
Manager   your room.

9 ṣaaḥibu   *Pronounce* : 'ar-raqm thalaathoon (4),
l-funduq   fi t-taabiqi th-thaalith

    Hotel   *English* : (The) number thirty (4), on the
Manager   third floor (in the floor the third).

10 ṣaaḥibu   *Pronounce* : hal maᶜak 'amtiᶜa ?
l-funduq

    Hotel   *English* : Have you (any) baggage ?
Manager

11 Jaak   *Pronounce* : naᶜam : haadhihi sh-shanta wahaadhihi l-ḥaqeeba l-kabeera

    Jack   *English* : Yes, this bag and this big suitcase.

NOTES

1   **Marhaban** (with the adverbial ending -an) is often pronounced simply **marhaba**. It has the same meaning as **'ahlan wasahlan** أَهْلاً وَسَهْلاً which we saw in Lesson 1.

2   You will recognize in the word **wahda** the same root as in the cardinal number "one", **waahid**. It is an adverb expressing the idea of oneness or aloneness, like the English "only". When a personal *oblique*-pronoun is attached to the end of it, it means "only I" (**wahdi**) or "only he" (**wahdahu**), and so on. And if the person needs emphasis, the pronoun may be inserted a second time, in its independent *subject* form, before **wahda**. This gives us :

Only I	'ana wahdi	أَنَا وَحْدِي
Only he	huwa wahdahu	هُوَ وَحْدَهُ
Only they	hum wahdahum	هُمْ وَحْدَهُمْ

But we may want to say, as in Sentence 6, *"for me alone"*. To do so, we merely prefix to **wahda**, with its attached object-pronoun (me, you, him, etc.), the preposition "for", **li**, with *its* attached oblique-pronoun (the same one). This gives us an expression meaning, literally, "for me, only me" or "for you, only you", etc. We can do the same with any of the object-pronouns. But notice that, before all pronouns other than "me", *li* becomes *la*.

For you [fem.] only	laki wahdaki	لَكِ وَحْدَكِ
For him only	lahu wahdahu	لَهُ وَحْدَهُ
For them only	lahum wahdahum	لَهُمْ وَحْدَهُمْ

We can also, of course, use other prepositions, so as to say, *"with you only", "from us only"*, and so on.

3   We have translated this sentence — **haadha huwa miftaah(u) ghurfatik** — as "Here is the key of your room", which is colloquial English for the situation. But it literally means "This it (is) the key of your room." The **huwa** ("it" in the masculine) can be dispensed with and often is. But colloquial Arabic prefers to repeat in this way the subject of the missing verb "is", almost as if the extra pronoun took its place.

4   For the explanation of "thirty", see the section on numbers below.

88

EXERCISES

١- هل غرفتك واسعة ؟

1 hal ghurfatuk waasi^ea ?
Is your room spacious ?

٢- أعطني مفتاحَ غرفتي

2 'a^etini miftaah(a) ghurfati
Give me the key of my room.

٣- كم غرفة عندكم في هذا الفندق؟

3 kam ghurfa ^eindakum fi haadha l-funduq ?
How many rooms have you in this hotel ?

كم عندكم من غرفة في هذا الفندق ؟

or
kam ^eindakum min ghurfa fi haadha l-funduq ?

٤- أُريدُ المفتاح حتّى أفتحَ غرفتي

4 'ureedu l-miftaah hatta 'aftaha ghurfati
I want the key (so as) to open my room.

٥- هل ترى غرفتَهُ ؟

5 hal tara ghurfatahu ?
Do you see his room ?

٦- هي في الطّابقِ الثّاني

6 hiya fi t-taabiqi th-thaani
It [fem.] is on the second floor.

89

GRAMMAR : Cardinal numbers

So as to let you stop spinning, we broke off at 10, in Lesson 15, our discussion of cardinal numbers. We will pick up with the round multiples of 10. The -ty words are all **masculine plural nouns**. With one exception, they are formed just by adding to the basic number (3, 4, 5, etc.), in its *masculine* form, the Arabic equivalent of the English -ty ending, which is **-oona** ون .

الدّرسُ الثّامِن عشر

'ad-darsu th-thaamin ᶜashar

في الفندق

١ـ عمر سيحمِلُ الأمتعـة إلى غرفتـك

The rest of the series, which we give in the table below, is more or less regular.
Notice in the table that the zero in Arabic is just a small dot, which may be round, oval or diamond-shaped.
Notice also that Arabic numbers containing more than one figure are written, unlike words, from left to right, just as in English. 1979 is *not* written 9791.

Multiples of 10

3	٣	thalaath	ثلاث	30	٣٠	thalaathoon(a)	ثلثون
4	٤	'arba$^\epsilon$	أربع	40	٤٠	'arba$^\epsilon$oon(a)	أربعون
5	٥	khams	خمس	50	٥٠	khamsoon(a)	خمسون
6	٦	sitt	ست	60	٦٠	sittoon(a)	ستون
7	٧	sab$^\epsilon$	سبع	70	٧٠	sab$^\epsilon$oon(a)	سبعون
8	٨	thamaanin	ثمان	80	٨٠	thamaanoon(a)	ثمانون
9	٩	tis$^\epsilon$	نسع	90	٩٠	tis$^\epsilon$oon(a)	تسعون
				100	١٠٠	mi'a(tun)	مائة

Lesson 18

The lesson the eighteenth

Pronounce : fi l-funduq
English : At (in) the hotel

1 saahibu   *Pronounce* : $^\epsilon$umar sayaḥmilu l'amti$^\epsilon$a
l-funduq   'ila ghurfatik
Hotel   *English* : Omar will carry the baggage
Manager   to your room.

91

٢ـ يا أُحمد! تعالَ معي حتّى
ترى غرفتي

(يأخذونَ المصعد و يصلون إلى الطّابقِ
الثّالث٥، جاك يعدُّ الأبواب)

٣ـ عشرة ـ خمسة عَشَرَ ـ عشرون ـ
خمسة وعشرون ©

٤ـ آه! ها هو الرّقم : ثلاثون ©

٥ـ و بابُ الغرفة مفتوح ...
تفضّل !

٦ـ شكرًا

٧ـ خذ ! هذا بخشيش لك .

٨ـ ألف © شكر، يا سيّدي !

2 Jaak 'ila
'aḥmad
Jack to
Ahmad

Pronounce : ya 'aḥmad ! ta$^\epsilon$aala ma$^\epsilon$i
ḥatta tara ghurfati
English : Ahmad ! Come with me to see
(in order that you see) my room.

(*Pronounce* : ya'khudhoona l-mis$^\epsilon$ad wayaṣiloon 'ila
t-taabiqi th-thaalith (1) ; jaak ya$^\epsilon$uddu l-'abwaab)
(*English* : They take the elevator and arrive at the third
floor (1) ; Jack reads off (counts) the numbers on the
doors.)

3 Jaak

Jack

Pronounce : $^\epsilon$ashra — khamsata $^\epsilon$ashara —
$^\epsilon$ishroon — khamsa wa$^\epsilon$ishroon (2)
English : Ten — fifteen — twenty —
twenty-five (2).

4 Jaak

Jack

Pronounce : 'aah ! ha huwa r-raqm :
thalaathoon (3)
English : Ah ! Here is number thirty (3).

5 Jaak

Jack

Pronounce : wabaabu l-ghurfa maftooḥ.
tafaddal
English : And the door of the room is
open. After you.

6 'aḥmad
Ahmad

Pronounce : shukran
English : Thank you.

7 Jaak 'ila
l-khaadim
Jack to the
bellboy

Pronounce : khudh ! haadha bakhsheesh
lak
English : Here (take) ! Here (is) a tip
for you.

8 'al-khaadim
The bellboy

Pronounce : 'alf (4) shukr, ya sayyidi
English : Thank you very much, sir (A
thousand (4) thanks, sir).

NOTES

All the notes in this lesson concern numbers. To simplify things, we will deal with the subject as a whole in the paragraphs below, rather than piecemeal. This will enable you to refer the specific details to an overall picture.

GRAMMAR : Cardinal Numbers

We dealt in Lesson 15 with the cardinal numbers up to 10, and in Lesson 17 with the multiples of 10 up to 100. We will back-track for a moment, before moving on, to look at a few basic principles.

Arabic noun-numbers can stand in one of three different relations with the words that follow them :

1 "Four joggers" is expressed : "*a* four[some] *of* joggers." The thing counted is here in the **oblique case** ("of") and in the **plural.** We have already seen this one.

2 "A hundred bingo-addicts" is expressed : "*a* hundred *of* [the species] bingo-addict." The thing counted is again in the **oblique case,** but this time in the **singular.**

3 "Nineteen candidates" is expressed : "nineteen candidate-wise." (This inelegant American turn of speech is very close to the Arabic.) Here the thing counted is in the **adverb case** and in the **singular.**

But we have already seen another kind of relation — one of **inverted gender** — between the numbers from 3 to 10 and the things they quantify. This inversion of gender holds whether the numbers are used alone (*seven* books) or in combinations (*seven*teen books. twenty-*seven* books). There is one exception, "ten", which in its combined forms (six-*teen*) breaks away from the upside-down principle.

Now we will pick up where we left off ; but we will leave aside for the moment 11 and 12.

1 The -teens, from 13 to 19. These conform to model 3 above ("nineteen candidate-wise") : the thing counted is in the **singular** and in the **adverb case.** The numbers themselves are formed in much the same way as the English -teens, but a bit more simply. That is, the "-teen" part of the number, in Arabic as in English, is a slightly modified "ten" (ᶜ**ashra(tun)** changes to ᶜ**ashara**) ; but the "three" part of "*thir*teen" remains "three", and the "five" part of "*fif*teen" remains "five".

94

What is tricky about these numbers is that one part of them, the "-teen" **agrees** in gender with the thing counted, while the other part, being one of the numbers from 3 to 9, **disagrees**.

Suppose we apply the above remarks to "thirteen children" :

(a) "Thirteen children" becomes "thirteen child-wise" (**adverb case**).

(b) The word for "child" being **masculine**, "three" must be **feminine**.

(c) For the same reason, "-teen" must be **masculine**.

And we come up with :

thalaathata ^ϵashara waladan   ثلاثـةَ عَشَرَ ولدًا

You will easily recognize here (a) the singular **walad** with its adverb case ending -**an** ; (b) the feminine ending in **taa' marboota** ة ‿ ـة on "three" ; and (c) the masculine "-teen", ^ϵ**ashara**.

If we now apply the same procedure to a *feminine* noun — "fifteen suitcases" — or "fifteen suitcase-wise" — the "five" part of the number becomes masculine in order to *dis*agree with the feminine "suitcase", while the "teen" part of it becomes feminine in order to *agree* with it :

khamsa ^ϵashrata ḥaqeebatan   خمسَ عَشْرَةَ حقيبة

2 Coming back now to 11 and 12. These are likewise -teens in Arabic (one-teen, two-teen). But, so far as gender is concerned, they are exceptions to what we have just finished saying : *both* parts of the number *agree* with the quantified noun. "Eleven children" [masculine], which becomes "one-teen child-wise", is thus :

'aḥada ^ϵashara waladan   أحدَ عَشَرَ ولدًا

And "twelve suitcase" [feminine], which becomes "two-teen suitcase-wise" is :

'ithnataa ^ϵashrata ḥaqeebatan   إثنتا عَشْرَةَ حقيبة

3 From 21 to 99. These numbers are formed on the old English model of "four-and-twenty blackbirds", the two parts of the number being connected as in English by "and", **wa**. "Five-and-twenty" is thus **khamsa(tun) wa**^ϵ**ishroona.**

But the blackbird pie remains distinctly Arabic. That is, the principles of gender and of case that we talked about in connections with the -teens apply in the same way to the numbers ending in -ty. "Twenty-six cars" [feminine] becomes "six-and-twenty car-wise" : **sitt(un) wa**^ϵ**ishroon sayyaara(tan).** Because "car" is feminine, "six" must be masculine. BUT the word for "twenty" is a masculine plural by nature and it remains that way regardless of the gender of the thing counted.

4 Round hundreds from 100 to 900. The word for "hundred" is a **feminine noun**. It remains **singular** for all the hundreds except 200. The things counted in hundreds are **singular nouns** in the **oblique case**, containing "of". Hence "100 dinars" is written :

A hundred of dinar **mi'a(tu) deenaar(in)** مائة دينار

or مئة دينار

200 (two hundreds), being a "dual", is formed by adding to the singular form, **mi'at**, the dual ending **-aani**. This gives us

mi'ataan(i), written : مائتان or مئتان

5 From 300 to 900, we merely put the words for 3, 4, 5 etc. in front of the word for "hundred" — in the **singular** exactly as in English, and in the **oblique case** ("of"). (As the oblique case ending is sloughed off in everyday speech, we don't show it.) "Five hundred francs", which we saw in Lesson 12, Sentence 8, is written "five of hundred of franc" : **khamsumi'a farank.** Here, then, are the hundreds :

300	thalaathumi'a	ثلثمائة
400	'arba$^\epsilon$umi'a	أربعمائة
500	khamsumi'a	خمسمائة
600	sittumi'a	ستّمائة
700	sab$^\epsilon$umi'a	سبعمائة
800	thamaaneemi'a	ثمانيمائة
900	tis$^\epsilon$umi'a	تسعمائة

6 1000, written **'alf,** is a **masculine singular noun** ("a thousand") and again takes a **singular** noun in the **oblique case**, containing "of". (As this oblique case ending is almost never pronounced, we don't show it.) We have an example of this in Sentence 8 above, where "a thousand thanks" is written :

A thousand of thank **'alf shukr** ألف شكر

Another and no less typically Arabic example is "a thousand and one nights", which becomes : "a thousand of night and a night" :

'alf layla walayla ألف ليلة وليلة

GRAMMAR : Ordinal Numbers

You have seen these at the head of every lesson, with their literal translations, so you know already that they behave like normal adjectives : they come *after* their nouns, *agree* with their nouns in gender and have the *definite article*. "The fourteenth lesson" is written :

The lesson the fourteenth   'ad-darsu r-raabi^ɛ ^ɛashar

Cardinal numbers

ORDINAL NUMBERS

		English	Masculine	Feminine
1	waahid	First	'awwal	'oola
2	'ithnaan	Second	thaanin	thaaniya
3	thalaatha	Third	thaalith	thaalitha
4	'arba^ɛa	Fourth	raabi^ɛ	raabi^ɛa
5	khamsa	Fifth	khaamis	khaamisa
6	sitta	Sixth	saadis	saadisa
7	sab^ɛa	Seventh	saabi^ɛ	saabi^ɛa
8	thamaaniya	Eighth	thaamin	thaamina
9	tis^ɛa	Ninth	taasi^ɛ	taasi^ɛa
10	^ɛashra	Tenth	^ɛaashir	^ɛaashira

EXERCISES

١ـ إلى أين أحمل أمتعتك ؟

1 'ila 'ayna 'aḥmil 'amti^ɛatak ?
   Where should I carry your baggage (To where I carry your baggage) ?

٢ـ ما هو رقم غرفتي ؟

2 ma huwa raqm(u) ghurfati ?
   What is my room number (the number of my room) ?

٣ـ الرّقم : تسعة و خمسون ، في الطّابق الخامس

3 'ar-raqm : tis^ɛa wakhamsoon, fi t-taabiqi l-khaamis
   Number 59, on the 5th floor (the number 9 and 50, in the floor the fifth).

٤ـ أعطني مفتاح غرفتي ، من فضلك

4 'a ^ɛtini miftaaḥ(a) ghurfati, min fadlik
   Give me the key to my room, please.

٥ـ مفتاحك في الباب

5 miftaahuk fi l-baab
   Your key is in the door.

GRAMMAR: Verbs
Pending aspect of CARRY (ḥamala) (Root : H-M-L)

I carry	'aḥmil	أَحْمِل
You [masc.] carry	taḥmil	تَحْمِل
You [fem.] carry	taḥmileena	تَحْمِلِين
He carries	yaḥmil	يَحْمِل
She carries	taḥmil	تَحْمِل
We carry	naḥmil	نَحْمِل
You carry	taḥmiloona	تَحْمِلُون
They carry	yaḥmiloona	يَحْمِلُون

الدَّرسُ التَّاسع عشر

ad-darsu t-tasi⁣ᵉ ⁣ᵉashar

في غرفةِ الفندق

١ـ أَغْلِقِ البابَ من فضلك !

٢ـ هذه غرفة جميلة

٣ـ نعم ، هي جميلة جِدًّا ...

ولكنَّ① الجوَّ فيها حارّ

98

The lesson the nineteenth

Pronounce : fi ghurfati l-funduq
English : In the hotel room (the room of the hotel)

1 Jaak
Jack
    Pronounce : 'aghliqi l-baab, min faḍlik
    English : Close the door, please.

2 'aḥmad
Ahmad
    Pronounce : haadhihi ghurfa jameela
    English : This (is an) attractive room.

3 Jaak

Jack
    Pronounce : naᶜam, hiya jameela jiddan...
walaakinna (1) l-jaww(a) feeha ḥaarr
    English : Yes, it [fem.] (is) very attractive... but (1) it's too warm (but the air in it is warm).

99

٤- صحيح ! سأفتح النّافذة

٥- أريد أن أغسل يديَّ

٦- أين الحمّام ؟

٧- وراءَك

(يغسل يديْهِ و يعود)

٨- هذه الغرفة تعجبُني

٩- ولكنَّ الفراشَ قريبٌ جدّاً⁽²⁾

منَ النّافذة

١٠- أنت تعبان⁽³⁾... إسترحْ !

4 'aḥmad   *Pronounce* : ṣaḥeeḥ ! sa'aftahu n-naafidha
    Ahmad   *English* : So it is ! I'll open the window.

5 Jaak   *Pronounce* : 'ureed 'an 'aghsila yadayya ["dual" form of yad, "hand"].
    Jack   *English* : I want to (that I) wash my hands.

6 Jaak   *Pronounce* : 'ayna l-hammaam ?
    Jack   *English* : Where (is) the bathroom ?

7 'aḥmad   *Pronounce* : waraa'ak
    Ahmad   *English* : Behind you.

(*Pronounce* : yaghsil(u) yadayhi waya$^\epsilon$ood)
(*English* : He washes his hands and comes back.)

8 Jaak   *Pronounce* : haadhihi l-ghurfa tu$^\epsilon$jibuni
    Jack   *English* : I like this room (this room pleases me).

9 Jaak   *Pronounce* : walaakinna l-firaash(a) qareeb(un) jiddan (2) mina n-naafidha
    Jack   *English* : But the bed (is) too (2) close to (from) the window.

10 'aḥmad   *Pronounce* : 'anta ta$^\epsilon$baan (3) ... 'istariḥ !
    Ahmad   *English* : You (are) tired (3) ... Have a rest.

NOTES

1 We have here a very curious feature of Arabic that is a bit tricky both to grasp and to explain. When the word "but" has the sense of "however" followed by a comma, it is written **laakin** لَكِنْ , often preceded by **wa**, and it behaves just as it would in English. For example :

However, he wants to open the door :
walaakin, yureed 'an yaftaḥa l-baab

However, she is beautiful :
walaakin, hiya jameela

و لكن ، هي جميلة

On the other hand, when the word has the sense just of a connecting "but" (rather than of "however" followed by a pause), it behaves as if it exerted a "butting" action on the word that comes after it. It is then written **laakinna** لَكِنَّ or **walaakinna**, and the word that is the object of this "butting" action goes into the object case.

Here are a couple of examples of this peculiar behaviour :

But her bed is far from the window.
walaakinna firaashaha | ba^ɛeed ^ɛani n-naafidha

و لكنَّ فراشَها بعيد عن النّافذة

But he washes his hands.
walaakinnahu yaghsil yadayhi

و لكنّهُ يغسل يديهِ

In the first example, the "butted" word, "bed", a definite noun, has the object case ending **-a**. In the second example, the "butted" word is the pronoun "he" (contained in the verb), which accordingly changes to "his", *hu*, attached to the end of **laakinna**. You are likely to crack your teeth on this until you become accustomed to it.

2 "Too", in Arabic, is expressed by the words for "very" or "extremely" :

It [masc.] (is) too far from here.
huwa ba^ɛeed jiddan ^ɛan huna

It [fem.] (is) too close to the door.

hiyya qareeba jiddan mina l-baab

3 Most of the adjectives we have seen until now have been formed by adding to the consonant root a vowel pattern made up of **a** plus **ee**, as in :

jameel	beautiful
qareeb	close
ba^ɛeed	distant, far

In the following list, we have some common adjectives which are formed by adding to the consonant root a pattern made up of **a** plus **aan**. Opposite the adjectives we give corresponding nouns

102

which are derived from the same conceptual root, but with several different vowel patterns. Keep in mind that, in Arabic, which is very unlike English in this respect, **most adjectives are not derived from nouns or vice versa : both are derived from a common root.**

Noun			Adjective		
Fatigue	ta$^\epsilon$ab	تعب	Tired	ta$^\epsilon$baan	تعبان
Thirst	$^\epsilon$atash	عطش	thirsty	$^\epsilon$atshaan	عطشان
Joy	faraḥ	فرح	Joyful	farḥaan	فرحان
Hunger	joo$^\epsilon$	جوع	Hungry	jaw$^\epsilon$aan	جوعان
Drunkenness	sukr	سكر	Drunk	sakraan	سكران
Sleepiness	nu$^\epsilon$aas	نعاس	Sleepy	na$^\epsilon$saan	نعسان

Adjectives having this characteristic vowel pattern are generally adjectives that describe a *state* or *condition* of body or mind ; and you will meet them most often in noun-sentences such as "I (am) tired" or "He (is) drunk".

EXERCISES

١- هل تريد أن أُغلقَ النّافذة ؟

1 hal tureed an 'ughliqa n-naafidha ?
Do you want me to (that I) close the window ?

٢- لا، أفضّل أن تفتحَ الباب

2 la, 'ufaddil 'an taftaḥa l-baab
No, I prefer that you open the door.

٣- الطّقس جميل في بلادك

3 'at taqs jameel fi bilaadik
The weather (is) fine in your country.

103

٤ـ نعم ، ولكنَّ الجوَّ حارٌّ جِدًّا

4 na⁣ᵉam. walaakinna l-jawwa ḥaarr(un) jiddan
   Yes, but it's very hot (the air is very hot).

٥ـ أُغلق غرفتَك و أعطني المفتاح

5 'aghliq ghurfatak wa'aᵉṭini l-miftaaḥ
   Close your room and give me the key.

٦ـ هلِ الفراش مريحٌ في غرفتي ؟

6 hali l-firaash mureeḥ fi ghurfati ?
   (Is) the bed comfortable in my room ?

٧ـ هل تريد أن تغسلَ يديْك ؟

7 hal tureed 'an taghsila yadayk ?
   Do you want to (that you) wash your hands ?

الدَّرسُ العشرون

'ad-darsu l-ᵉishroon

في غرفـةِ الفندق
(أحمد يمدُّ ورقـة إلى جمَّاك)

١ـ تفضَّل ! هذا عنواني و هذا
رقمُ هاتفي

104

GRAMMAR : Verbs

More common verbs in the indicative of the **pending aspect** (singular only). (We omit this time the feminine forms, as you now know that, in the second person, they end in **-eena** and that, in the third person, they are identical with the second person of the masculine.)

WASH (ghasala)	(Root : GH-S-L)	
I wash	'aghsilu	أَغسِل
You wash	taghsilu	تغسِل
He washes	yaghsilu	يغسِل

OPEN (fataha)	(Root : F-T-Ḥ)	
I open	'aftaḥu	أفتَح
You open	taftaḥu	تفتَح
He opens	yaftaḥu	يفتَح

CLOSE (aghlaqa)	(Root : GH-L-Q)	
I close	'ughliqu	أغلِق
You close	tughliqu	تغلِق
He closes	yughliqu	يغلِق

Lesson 20

The lesson the twentieth

Pronounce : fi ghurfati l-funduq
English : In the hotel room

(Pronounce : 'aḥmad yamuddu waraqa 'ila Jaak)
(English : Ahmad hands a piece of paper to Jack.)

1 'aḥmad	*Pronounce* : tafaḍḍal ; haadha ᶜunwaani wahaadha raqm(u) haatifi
Ahmad	*English* : Here. This (is) my address and this (is) my telephone number.

105

٢- على كلِّ حالٍ ، سوف أُخابِرُكَ
غدًا

٣- لِكَيْ[1] نزورَ المدينةَ معًا

٤- شكرًا ... ولكن ، قد[2] أُزعِجك ؟

٥- لا ، على العكس : غدًا هو
يومُ[3] الجمعة

٦- لا أعمل ... والآن ، أترُكُكَ
لِتستريحَ

٧- و أتمنّى لكَ ليلةً سعيدة

106

2 'aḥmad

Ahmad

Pronounce : ^εala kulli ḥaal, sawfa 'ukhaa-biruk(a) ghadan

English : In any case, I'll phone you tomorrow.

3 'aḥmad

Ahmad

Pronounce : likay (1) nazoora l-madeena ma^εan

English : So that (1) we may visit the town together.

4 Jaak

Jack

Pronounce : shukran ... walaakin, qad (2) 'uz^εijuk ?

English : Thank you ... but perhaps (2) I'll be bothering you.

5 'aḥmad

Ahmad

Pronounce : la, ^εala l-^εaks ; ghadan, huwa yawmu l-jumu^εa (3)

English : No, on the contrary ; tomorrow it (is) Friday (3).

6 'aḥmad

Ahmad

Pronounce : la 'a^εmal ... wal'aan 'atrukuk(a) litastareeḥa

English : I don't work ... And now I'll leave you to (so that you may) have a rest.

7 'aḥmad

Ahmad

Pronounce : wa'atamanna lak(a) layla(tan) sa^εeeda

English : And I wish you a good (happy) night.

٨ ‑ إلى اللّقاءِ غدًا ④ إن شاء الـلّـه !

٩‑ إلى اللّقاء ... و شكرًا

NOTES

1 Notice, in Sentence 3, the use of the conjunction **likay,**(mean-

ing "so that" or "in order that") لكَيْ followed by a verb in
the subjunctive, as previously mentioned in Review Lesson 14.

2 We saw in Lesson 6 the use of **qad** قد with a verb in the
completed aspect. Used as it is here before a verb in the **pending
aspect**, it has the sense of "perhaps", much like the full word for

"perhaps" or "maybe", **rubbama** ربّما in Lessons 12
and 13.

3 At the end of this lesson you will find the names in Arabic
of the days of the week. Other time-words are :

Today	'al yawm(a)	اليوم
Yesterday	'ams	أمس
or	'al-baariha(ta)	ألبارحة
Tomorrow	ghadan	غدًا

4 The literal sense of **'ila l-liqaa'(i)** is "to (i.e. until) the meeting".
We saw in Lesson 11 another common form of good-bye, **maᵉa
s-salaama.**

EXERCISES

١‑ ما هو رقمُ هاتفِك ؟

1 ma huwa raqm(u) haatifik ?
What is your telephone number ?

108

8 'aḥmad *Pronounce* : 'ila l-liqaa'(i) (4) ghadan, 'in shaa'a l-Ilaah !

Ahmad *English* : Good-bye (4), I'll see you tomorrow, I hope (if God wishes).

9 Jaak *Pronounce* : 'ila l-liqaa' ... washukran
English : Good-bye ... and thank you.

*

٢ ـ الرّقمُ : خمسمائة وثلاثة وعشرون

2 'ar-raqm : khamsumi'a wathalaatha waᶜishroon
The number five hundred twenty-three (five hundred and three and twenty).

٣ ـ خابرني غدًا في المكتب

3 khaabirni ghadan fi l-maktab
Phone me tomorrow at the office.

٤ ـ هل تعمل يومَ الخميس ؟

4 hal taᶜmal yawma l-khamees ?
Do you work on Thursday ?

٥ ـ ماذا تعمل غدًا ؟

5 maadha taᶜmal ghadan ?
What are you doing tomorrow ?

٦ ـ سأكونُ في الفندقِ غدًا

6 sa'akoon(u) fi l-funduq(i) ghadan
I'll be at the hotel tomorrow.

GRAMMAR : Days of the week

The names of the days of the week are derived (except for Friday) from the same roots as the names of the cardinal numbers. Sunday, for example, is "Day the one", Monday is "Day the two", and so on. Friday, the Moslem sabbath, is "Meeting day". But the numbers here have slightly different forms than when they are used as such. We give you below the complete and the shortened versions of the names of days.

	Full	Shortened	
Sunday	yawmu l-'aḥad	'al-'aḥad	الأحد
Monday	yawmu l-'ithnayn	'al-'ithnayn	الإثنين
Tuesday	yawmu th-thulaathaa'	'ath-thulaathaa'	الثّلثاء
Wednesday	yawmu l-'arbi$^\epsilon$aa'	'al-'arbi$^\epsilon$aa'	الأربعاء
Thursday	yawmu l-khamees	'al-khamees	الخميس
Friday	yawmu l-jumu$^\epsilon$a	'al-jumu$^\epsilon$a	الجمعة
Saturday	yawmu s-sabt	'as-sabt	السّبت

والآن أتركك لتستريح .

110

GRAMMAR : Verbs

A few more common verbs, again in the **pending aspect, indicative, singular only.** (See introductory remark on page 105.)

VISIT (zaara) (Root : Z-W-R)

I visit — 'azooru — أزور

You visit — tazooru — تزور

He visits — yazooru — يزور

WORK (ᶜamila) (Root : ᶜ-M-L)

I work — 'aᶜmalu — أعمل

You work — taᶜmalu — تعمل

He works — yaᶜmalu — يعمل

TELEPHONE (khaabara) (Root : KH-B-R)

I telephone — 'ukhaabiru — أخابر

You telephone — tukhaabiru — تخابر

He telephones — yukhaabiru — يخابر

LEAVE (taraka) (someone or something) (Root : T-R-K)

I leave — 'atruku — أترك

You leave — tatruku — تترك

He leaves — yatruku — يترك

REST ('istaraaha) (Root : R-W-H)

I rest — 'astareehu — أستريح

You rest — tastareehu — تستريح

He rests — yastareehu — يستريح

Rest ! [Imperative, masculine singular] 'istarih — إسترح!

111

مراجعة

If you have not dealt before with a highly inflected language such as German or Latin or Greek, the feature of Arabic that is probably giving you the most trouble is the system of **cases**. As for **numbers**, they are almost certainly causing you to gnash your teeth. We will therefore take another look at both these matters before going on to a few that are less troublesome.

1 Cases. You can get by, in *spoken* Arabic, without having mastered these, as case-endings are for the most part either slurred over or dropped in everyday speech. But if you don't know them, you will find it very hard, in *written* Arabic, to grasp how words hang together in a sentence, how they "work" and why they behave as they do. Here, in very simple terms, is practically everything that you need to know :

Nouns (and words assimilated to them) have various functions in a sentence, called "cases", which are identified by corresponding short-vowel endings added to them. There are only three cases, each having its own short vowel :

(a) A noun is in the **subject case** when it is the subject of the verb (whether the verb is expressed or, as in noun-sentences, merely implied). In "The car hit the tree", the subject is "the car". The subject case ending is **-u** when the noun is **definite** (whether because it is preceded by the definite article "the" or because the grammatical structure, such as that of the "yoked" couple", makes it so). When the noun is **indefinite**, **-u** becomes **-un**. For example :

The lesson	'ad-darsu
A lesson	darsun

The lesson the first and the twentieth

Pronounce : muraaja$^\epsilon$a
English : Review

(b) A noun is in the **object case** when it is the object of the verb. In "The car hit the tree", the object of the verb is "the tree". The object case ending is **-a** when the noun is **definite, -an** when **indefinite.** For example :

Give me *the* cigarette   'a$^\epsilon$tini s-seejaarata

Give me *a* cigarette   'a$^\epsilon$tini seejaaratan

But keep in mind that certain verbs which in English would not take objects — *was, remain, become,* etc. — do take them in Arabic :

He *was* small   kaana sagheeran   كان صغيرًا

The full name of this case is really the **object/adverb case** (and we often refer to it as either one or the other). The reason is that this case also has an adverbial function : it is used to make nouns say (for example) *where, when* or *how.* The adverbial case ending is most often **-an.** Here are a few common instances of this :

The evening	'al masaa'u	المساء
(In) the evening	masaa'an	مساءً
The morning	'as-sabaahu	الصباح
(In) the morning	sabaahan	صباحًا
Gratitude	shukrun	شكر
With gratitude (= Thank you)	shukran	شكرًا
Natural disposition	tab$^\epsilon$un	طبع
Naturally (= Of course)	tab$^\epsilon$an	طبعًا

113

(c) A noun is in the **oblique case** when it is **governed by a preposition** (on, with, towards, etc.) or when it **contains** the implied preposition "of" (which is thus an unnecessary word in Arabic). The indirect case ending is -i when the noun is **definite** and -in when **indefinite** :

In the airplane	fi t-taa'irati
To the airport	'ila l-mataari
For a child	liwaladin
The door *of the* hotel	baabu l-funduqi

As you see, cases are in fact a fairly simple matter — a great deal simpler than the grammatical terms needed to talk about them.

2 Numbers Your English dictionary will probably define a giraffe as a ruminant quadruped mammal with a long neck. But, unless there is a picture beside the definition, this will not help you much to visualize a giraffe if you have never seen one. The giraffe we are dealing with, the Arabic system of numbers, is in fact a very odd beast. So as to give you a clearer **picture** of what it is, leaving aside definitions and rules, we give you on pages 116-117 a simple table that will enable you to see at a glance how Arabic numbers work. In the English columns of this table, **everything in bold-face type is masculine** ; *everything in italics is feminine,* and EVERYTHING IN CAPITALS IS PLURAL OR DUAL. As for case endings, you will immediately recognize in the transcribed Arabic columns the oblique case -**in** and the adverb case -**an**.

There is a great deal more to be said about Arabic numbers, but most of it can wait. For now, we will make just a few additional comments :

(a) The word "one", when used as an adjective ("one child", "one woman") is **waahid** [masc.] or **waahida** [fem.]. But when it is used as a *noun* (as in "one of the sailors"), it changes its form and becomes **'ahad(un)** [masc.] or **'ihda** [fem.]. It is this noun-form of the word that is combined with "ten" to make "eleven" (or "one-teen") : **'ahada $^\epsilon$ashara** [masc.] and **'ihda $^\epsilon$ashrata** [fem.].

114

(b) The noun form of "one", **'aḥad(un)** is also used to mean "someone" or "something" in negative sentences such as "I didn't see someone" — **ma ra'aytu 'aḥad(an)** — which we would of course translate as "I didn't see *anyone*".

(c) We have said that the "dual" ending of numbers (and of nouns in general) is **-aan(i).** This is in fact the ending of the subject case. In the object/adverb case and the oblique case, it is **-ayn(i).** For example, *"with* two children" is written **maᶜa waladayn(i).**

(d) All the -ty numbers (20, 30, etc.) take the case ending that is required by the job they do in a sentence. Their subject case ending is **-oona** ; in the object/adverb case *and* in the oblique case, they end in **-eena.** For example :

Give me twenty books   **'aᶜtini ᶜishreena kitaab(an)**

(e) You are probably wondering how the various "rules" that we have given for Arabic numbers apply to such composite numbers as 603 or 715. This is in fact very simple : the part of the composite number that changes its gender to agree or disagree with the gender of the thing quantified is not the 600 or the 700 but the 3 or the 15.

ليلة سعيدة

115

NUMBERS with a masculine noun : child — CHILDREN (walad - 'awlaad)

a	1 a child one	walad waahid
b	2 CHILDREN TWO	waladaani thnaani [dual]
c	3 - 10 *four* of CHILDREN *ten* of CHILDREN	'arba$^\epsilon$atu 'awlaadin $^\epsilon$ashratu 'awlaadin
d	11 one-teen child [wise] 12 two-teen child [wise]	'ahada $^\epsilon$ashara waladan 'ithnaa $^\epsilon$ashara waladan
e	13 - 19 *thir*-teen child[wise] *six~*teen child[wise]	thalaathata $^\epsilon$ashara waladan sittata $^\epsilon$ashara waladan
f	20 - 30 - 40... 90 **THIRTY** child[wise]	thalaathoona waladan

g	21 - 22 - 23... 29
	31 - 32 - 33... 39
	Etc.
	
	four-AND-TWENTY child[wise]
	    'arba$^\epsilon$atun wa$^\epsilon$ishroona waladan
	seven-AND-FORTY child[wise]
	    sab$^\epsilon$atun wa'arba$^\epsilon$oona waladan

h	100 a hundred of [the species] child	mi'atu waladin
i	200 TWO *HUNDREDS* of [the species] child	mi'ataa waladin
j	300 - 400 - 500... 900 *five* of hundred of [the species] child	thalaathu mi'ati waladin
k	1000 a thousand of [the species] child	'alf waladin

NUMBERS with a feminine noun : lady — LADIES (sayyida - sayyidaat)

1 *a lady one*	sayyidatun waaḥida	**a**
2 *LADIES TWO*	sayyidataani thnataani [dual]	**b**
3 - 10 **four** *of LADIES* **ten** *of LADIES*	'arba^εu sayyidaatin ^εashru sayyidaatin	**c**
11 *one-teen lady* [wise] 12 *two-teen lady* [wise]	'ihda ^εashrata sayyidatan 'ithnataa ^εashrata sayyidatan	**d**
13 - 19 **thir**-*teen lady* [wise] **six**-*teen lady* [wise]	thalaatha ^εashrata sayyidatan sitta ^εashrata sayyidatan	**e**
20 - 30 - 40... 90 **THIRTY** *lady* [wise]	thalaathoona sayyidatan	**f**

21 - 22 - 23... 29
31 - 32 - 33... 39
Etc.
 	
four-*AND-TWENTY lady* [wise]
   'arba^εun wa^εishroona sayyidatan
seven-*AND-FORTY lady* [wise]
   sab^εun wa'arba^εoona sayyidatan
		g

100 *a hundred* *of* [the species] *lady*	mi'atu sayyidatin	**h**
200 *TWO HUNDREDS* *of* [the species] *lady*	mi'ataa sayyidatin	**i**
300 - 400 - 500... 900 **five** *of hundred* *of* [the species] *lady*	thalaathu mi'ati sayyidatin	**J**
1000 *a thousand* *of* [the species] *lady*	'alf sayyidatin	**k**

3 Verbal nouns. We have already met many of these but have not yet called them by their grammatical name. You are perfectly familiar with them in English and take them for granted. They are even more common in Arabic. Here are some examples. We show in parentheses what happens to them in Arabic : they almost always take the definite article, "the", whereas in English they often don't. In any event, they are always *definite* nouns, definiteness being imposed on them, if not by the article, then by other words with which they are grammatically combined (in "yoked couples"), such as possessive pronouns ("my", "his", "your", etc.). We give the examples in English only so as to make clear the principle of the thing :

(The) no **parking**	The **reporting** of an event
(The) no **smoking**	My **wanting** to go

الدَّرسُ الثّاني و العشرون

'ad-darsu th-thaani wa l-⁶ishroon

في غرفةِ الفندق

(يُطْرَقُ الباب)

١ ـ تفضّل !

٢ ـ عفواً ⁽¹⁾، يا سيّدي ؛
أُلَ ⁽²⁾ أزعجك ؟

118

The **hunting** of the snark	Your **leaving** early
The **writing** of a novel	Your **forgetting** me

Many nouns that don't *look* "verbal" in English are explicitly so in Arabic :

The **visit**(ing)	The **fight**(ing)
The **tour**(ing)	The **welcom**(ing)
The **grasp**(ing)	The **disregard**(ing)

We will see later how verbal nouns are formed from verbs — or, more exactly, how verbs and verbal nouns are formed from the same root. For now, just keep in mind what a verbal noun is.

⸻

Lesson 22

The lesson the second and the twentieth

⸻

Pronounce : fi ghurfati l-funduq

English : In the hotel room

(*Pronounce* : yutraqu l-baab)
(*English* : There is a knock at the door [Is knocked the the door].)

1	Jaak	*Pronounce* : tafaddal !
	Jack	*English* : Come in !

2	'al khaadim	*Pronounce* : [€]afwan (1), ya sayyidi ; 'ala 'uz[€]ijuk (2) ?
	The valet	*English* : Excuse me (1), sir ; I'm not disturbing you (2) ?

119

٣ـ لا ، أبدًا ④

٤ـ هل أنت في حاجة ④ إلى

شيء ؟

٥ـ لا ، شكرًا ، كلُّ شيءٍ على ما

يُرام

٦ـ هل تعجبُك ⑤ هذه الغرفة ؟

٧ـ نعم ، هي ممتازة ...

٨ـ ولكن ، يصل إليها

بعضُ الضّجيج

3 Jaak   *Pronounce* : la, 'abadan (3)

Jack   *English* : No, not at all (3).

4 'al khaadim   *Pronounce* : hal 'anta fi ḥaaja (4) 'ila shay' ?

The valet   *English* : Do you need (are you in need of) (4) something ?

5 Jaak   *Pronounce* : la, shukran, kullu shay'(in) ᶜala ma yuraam

Jack   *English* : No, thank you. Everything (is) fine (as wanted).

6 'al khaadim   *Pronounce* : hal tuᶜjibuk (5) haadhihi l-ghurfa ?

The valet   *English* : Do you like (5) this room (does this room please you) ?

7 Jaak   *Pronounce* : naᶜam, hiya mumtaaza ...

Jack   *English* : Yes, it is first-rate (excellent)...

8 Jaak   *Pronounce* : walaakin, yaṣil 'ilayha baᶜdu d-dajeej

Jack   *English* : But it's a little noisy (arrives to it some noise).

121

٩- و الفراش قريبٌ جدّاً
منَ النّافذة

١٠- هل تريد غرفةً أخرى؟ ⑥

١١- لا ، على كلِّ حال ، أنا
تعبان ، سأنامُ بسرعة ⑦

NOTES

1 We have already met (in Lesson 2) ^εafwan عفواً in the sense of "You're welcome" or "Don't mention it", when used as a reply to "Thank you". Here it is used in the sense of "Sorry" or "Excuse me" or "I beg your pardon". You are likely to encounter it also in |the form of the noun (with its definite article), 'al ^εafwu العفو , which means literally "the pardon".

2 There are two things to note here :

(a) When the interrogative **hal** is followed by a word beginning with ‌ا, as in the case here, it is customarily replaced, for euphonic reasons, by the word **'a**. Here, therefore **hal la** هل لا؟ becomes **'a la** أ لا ؟ .

(b) The valet uses, as is customary, the singular "you" when he says to Jack (who is alone), " Am I disturbing you ?" : hal 'uz^εijuk ?

هل أزعجُك ؟

122

9 Jaak   *Pronounce* : wal-firaash qareeb(un) jiddan
                    mina n-naafidha

Jack   *English* : And the bed (is) too close to
                    (very close from) the window.

10 'al khaadim   *Pronounce* : hal tureed ghurfa(tan)
                    'ukhra (6) ?

The valet   *English* : Do you want another (6) room ?

11 Jaak   *Pronounce* : la, $^\epsilon$ala kulli ḥaal, 'ana
                    ta$^\epsilon$baan, sa'anaam(u) bisur$^\epsilon$a (7)

Jack   *English* : No, in any case, I'm tired ;
                    I'll be asleep in no time (I shall sleep
                    with speed) (7).

He might very well, as a sign of deference, [see Lesson 2, Note 2],
make use of the plural "you" : hal 'uz$^\epsilon$ijukum هل أزعجكم ؟
But this would require that he continue to use it for the rest of the
conversation, which would make things a bit *too* deferential and
stiff.

3 The word **'abadan** literally means "never" as opposed to "always", which is **daa'iman** دائمًا . But, as in English, it is also

used to mean "not at all", or "not in the least" or "absolutely
not". In colloquial English we similarly say, "Never a whit the
wiser" or "Never on your life".

4 "Need" can be rendered either by the corresponding Arabic
verb (**'iḥtaaja** plus the preposition **'ila**), which we saw on page
65, or by the Arabic expression corresponding to "be in need of",
which is used here.

123

"I need" can thus be written either 'aḥtaaj 'ila أَحْتاج إلى ,
or, as you see below, with a noun-phrase :

أَنا في حاجةٍ إلى

I (am) in (the) need of   'ana fi ḥaaja 'ila

أَنتَ في حاجةٍ إلى

You (are) in (the) need of   'anta fi ḥaaja 'ila

هو في حاجةٍ إلى

He (is) in (the) need of   huwa fi ḥaaja 'ila

5 In a normal Arabic sentence, of which this is an example, the verb comes first. (Here it is preceded only by the interrogative **hal**, which is essentially a question mark rather than a word). Literally this sentence says, "Pleases you the room ?" (Under the influence of dialects, the practice of putting the verb first is sometimes disregarded ; but you would do well to respect it.) **When the verb comes first and has an expressed subject ("the room"), it is always in the singular, even if its subject is plural.** (Here the verb would remain as it is even if its subject were "the rooms".)

6 "Room" being a feminine noun, its adjective "(an)other" is likewise feminine : **'ukhra** أُخْرى . The masculine form of this adjective is **'aakhar** آخَر .

7 The expression **bisur∈a**, meaning literally "with speed" (hence "quickly" or "rapidly") is made up of the preposition **bi** بِ , meaning "with", plus **sur∈a**, "speed". This preposition **bi** has many different uses, most of which ressemble closely enough English uses of "with" so that they require no grammatical explanation. But note carefully the following examples and shades of meaning :

(a)   I speak with difficulty.
         'atakallam biṣu∈ooba   أَتكلّم بِصعوبة

(b)   I will sleep with speed (quickly)
         sa'anaam(u) bisur∈a   سأنام بِسرعة

124

(c)   I want coffee with milk (i.e. combined with milk)
'ureed qahwa biḥaleeb

أريد قهوة بِحليب

(d)   He came with the plane (i.e. by plane)
waṣala biṭ-ṭaa'ira

وصل بِالطّائرة

(e)   Are we going with the car (i.e. by car)
hal nadhhab bis-sayyaara ?

هل نذهب بِالسيّارة ؟

(f)   I live with this town (i.e. in it)
'askun bihaadhihi l-madeena

أسكن بهذه المدينة.

[Note that in this instance **bi** is used instead of **fi**, "in".]

EXERCISES

١- هذا الفندق يعجبني

1 **haadha l-funduq yuᶜjibuni**
I like this hotel (This hotel pleases me).

٢- هذه الغرفة تعجبني

2 **haadhihi l-ghurfa tuᶜjibuni**
I like this room (This room pleases me).

٣- هل يعجبك بلدي ؟

3 **hal yuᶜjibuk baladi ?**
Do you like my country (Does my country please you) ?

٤- هل تعجبك المدينة ؟

4 **hal tuᶜjibuki l-madeena ?**
Do you like the city (Does the city please you) ?

٥- هذا يعجبنا

5 **haadha yuᶜjibuna**
We like this (This pleases us).

٦- هل يعجبكم هذا ؟

6 **hal yuᶜjibukum haadha ?**
Do you [plur.] like this (Does this please you) ?

125

GRAMMAR : Verbs

The **indicative**, in the **pending aspect**, of **SLEEP (naama)**
(Root : N-W-M)

I sleep	'anaamu	أنام
You [masc.] sleep	tanaamu	تنام
You [fem.] sleep	tanaameena	تنامين
He sleeps	yanaamu	ينام
She sleeps	tanaamu	تنام

الدّرسُ الثّالثُ والعشرونَ

'ad-darsu th-thaalith wal-ᶜishroon

في غرفةِ الفندق

١ـ سآخذ حمّامًا

٢ـ هل يُوجد① ماءٌ ساخن
في هذه السّاعة ؟

٣ـ طبعًا ؛ ألماءُ السّاخن
موجودٌ© دائمًا عندنا

126

The lesson the third and the twentieth

Pronounce : fi ghurfati l-funduq
English : In the hotel room

1 Jaak 'ila   *Pronounce* : sa'aakhudh ḥammaam(an)
l-khaadim
Jack to   *English* : I shall take a bath.
the valet

2 Jaak 'ila   *Pronounce* : hal yoojad (1) maa'(un)
l-khaadim   saakhin, fi haadhihi s-saa$^{\epsilon}$a ?
Jack to   *English* : Is there (1) hot water at this
the valet   hour ?

3 'al khaadim   *Pronounce* : tab$^{\epsilon}$an ; 'al maa'u s-saakhin
mawjood(un) (2) daa'iman $^{\epsilon}$indana
The valet   *English* : Of course ; there is (2) always
hot water here (in our place).

٤- طيِّب ! هل يمكن(٣) أن أتعشَّى
في الفندق ؟

٥- هذا غير ممكن(٤)، يا سيِّدي ؛
نقدِّمُ الفطور فقط

٦- أين يمكن أن أتعشَّى ؟

٧- أعرف مطعمًا ممتازًا ،
قريبًا(٥) من هنا

٨- إسمُهُ : « مطعمُ الواحة»

٩- سترى ؛ هناك يقدِّمون(٦)
طعامًا لذيذًا و رخيصًا

4 Jaak

Pronounce : ṭayyib ! hal yumkin (3) 'an 'ata^ϵashsha fi l-funduq ?

Jack

English : Fine. Could (is it possible that) (3) I have dinner at the hotel ?

5 'al khaadim

Pronounce : haadha ghayr mumkin (4), ya sayyidi, nuqaddimu l-futoor faqaṭ

The valet

English : It's not possible (4) (this is not possible), sir ; we serve breakfast only.

6 Jaak

Pronounce : 'ayna yumkin 'an 'ata^ϵashsha ?

Jack

English : Where could I have dinner ?

7 'al khaadim

Pronounce : 'a^ϵrif maṭ^ϵam(an) mumtaaz(an), qareeban (5) min huna

The valet

English : I know an excellent restaurant close by (5).

8 'al khaadim

Pronounce : 'ismuhu maṭ^ϵamu l-waaḥa

The valet

English : Its name (is) the Oasis Restaurant (the Restaurant of the Oasis).

9 'al khaadim

Pronounce : satara ; hunaaka yuqaddimoona (6) ṭa^ϵaam(an) ladheedh(an) warakhees(an)

The valet

English : You will see ; they serve (6) delicious and inexpensive food there (there they serve...).

129

١٠ـ أَشْكُرُكَ ... وَالآنَ، سَآخُذُ حَمَّامِي قَبْلَ العَشَاءِ

١١ـ وَأَنْزِلُ بَعْدَ سَاعَةٍ تَقْرِيبًا

١٢ـ طَيِّبٌ، يَا سَيِّدِي!

*

NOTES

1 You will recall from Lesson 13, Note 1, that "Is there ?" can be expressed either by **hal yoojad**, as it is here, or by **hal hunaaka**

هَلْ هُنَاكَ؟

2 Here is a third way of saying "There is" (or "Is there ?", as the case may be) : **mawjood**. This is in fact the passive participle ("being found") of the verb **wajada** ("he found"), which, in its pending

aspect (passive) gives **yoojad** يُوجَد , meaning "he (or it) is found", hence "exists" or "is present".

3 The usual way of saying "Can I ?" or "May I ?" is : "Is it possible that... ? " followed by a clause with a verb in the subjunctive, as explained in Lesson 14.

130

10 Jaak   *Pronounce* : 'ashkuruk... wal'aan
                  sa'aakhudh hammaami qabla l-ᶜashaa'
      Jack   *English* : (I) thank you... And now,
                  I'll take my bath before dinner.

11 Jaak   *Pronounce* : wa'anzil (7) baᶜda saaᶜa
                  taqreeban
      Jack   *English* : I'll be down (7) in about an
                  hour (I'll go down after an hour about).

12 al khaadim *Pronounce* : ṭayyib, ya sayyidi !
      The valet   *English* : Very good, sir.

For example, "May I smoke ?" becomes "Is it possible that I
smoke ?", which is written : hal yumkin 'an 'udakhkhina ?

هل يمكن أن أُدَّخَّنَ ؟

4 "Possible", in Arabic, is **mumkin**   ممكن   . "It (is)

possible" is written : **haadha mumkin**   هذا ممكن   . This

phrase can not be made negative just by adding the word for "not",
la. The negative is formed, instead, in one of two ways :

(a) By using the word **ghayr**   غير   , which literally means
"other than". Thus, "It is not possible" becomes : "It (is) other
than possible" : **haadha ghayr mumkin**   هذا غير ممكن

(b) By using the verb "not to be", which we will discuss later, and which, like "to be", is an active (transitive) verb that takes a direct object, as explained in Lesson 14.

5 qareeban قَرِيبًا is the *adverb* for "close by" or "near by" not a preposition. Notice the adverbial ending, **-an**.

6 Arabic, like English, makes common use of the impersonal "they", corresponding to "one" in British usage. Here we have : *They serve* inexpensive food" :

yuqaddimoon(a) ta$^\epsilon$aam(an) rakhees(an)

يقدّمون طعامًا رخيصًا

But the same thing can also be said — again as in English — with a passive construction : "Delicious food *is served*" : **yuqaddam ta$^\epsilon$aam ladheedh**

يقدّم طعامٌ لذيذ

This passive construction can be used only when no agent is expressed. That is, you can not say in Arabic : "Delicious food is served *by* someone". If you want to express the agent, you must go back to the active construction, "They serve..."

7 Notice that the pending aspect of the verb clearly enough expresses the future so that the particle **sa** is not needed.

EXERCISES

١ـ هل تقدّمونَ العشاءَ هنا ؟

1 hal tuqaddimoona l-$^\epsilon$ashaa'(a) huna ?
Do you [plural] serve dinner here ?

٢ـ هل يمكن أن نزورَ المدينةَ اليومَ ؟

2 hal yumkin 'an nazoora l-madeena l-yawm(a) ?
Can we (Is it possible that we) visit the city today ?

132

٣ـ هذا غير ممكن، أنا أعمل حتى
القَّادسة والرّبع مساءً

3 haadha ghayr mumkin, 'ana 'a^εmal ḥatta s-saadisa
war-rub^ε(i) masaa'an
It (this is) not possible. I work till a quarter past six
(the sixth and the quarter in the evening).

٤ـ هل تريد أن تتعشى معنا في المطعم؟

4 hal tureed 'an tata^εashsha ma^εana fi l-mat^εam ?
Do you [sing.] want to (that you) dine with us in the
restaurant ?

٥ـ بكلِّ سرور؛ آخذ حمّامًا وأنزل
بعد عشرين دقيقة

5 bikulli suroor ; 'aakhudh ḥammaam(an) wa'anzil ba^εda
^εishreen daqeeqa
With (all) pleasure ; I'll take a bath and I'll be down in
twenty minutes.

ساخذ حمّاما

GRAMMAR : Verbs

The **indicative**, in the **pending aspect**, of three more verbs (singular only).

GO DOWN or COME DOWN (nazala) (Root : N-Z-L)

I go down	'anzilu	أنزل
You [masc.] go down	tanzilu	تنزل
You [fem.] go down	tanzileena	تنزلين
He goes down	yanzilu	ينزل

الدّرسُ الرّابعُ والعشرون

'ad-darsu r-raabiᶜ wal-ᶜishroon

في غرفةِ الفندق

١ـ في أيّةِ ساعةٍ تريد أن أقدّمَ
لكَ الفطور صباحَ غدٍ⁅⁆ ؟

134

SERVE (qaddama) (in the sense of "present" or "offer")
(Root : Q-D-M)

I serve	'uqaddimu	أُقَدِّم
You [masc.] serve	tuqaddimu	تُقَدِّم
You [fem.] serve	tuqaddimeena	تُقَدِّمِي
He serves	yuqaddimu	يُقَدِّم

DINE (ta$^\epsilon$ashsha) (Root : $^\epsilon$-SH-Y)

I dine	'ata$^\epsilon$ashsha	أَتَعَشَّى
You [masc.] dine	tata$^\epsilon$ashsha	تَتَعَشَّى
You [fem.] dine	tata$^\epsilon$ashshayna	تَتَعَشَّيْ
He dines	yata$^\epsilon$ashsha	يَتَعَشَّى

Lesson 24

The lesson the fourth and the twentieth

Pronounce : fi ghurfati l-funduq
English : In the hotel room

1 'al khaadim	*Pronounce* : fi 'ayyati saa$^\epsilon$a tureed 'an 'uqaddima laka l-futoor, ṣabaaḥa ghad (1) ?
The valet	*English* : At what time do you want me to (that I) serve you breakfast tomorrow morning (1) ?

135

٢- في الثّامنة و النّصف[٥] ، مِن فضلك !

٣- طيّب ! وماذا تفضّل لِلفطور ؟

٤ - هل تريد قهوة أم[٣] حليبًا أم شاي ؟

٥ - أعطني قهوة بِحليب[٤]

٦- مع خبز و زبدة و عسل .

٧ - تحت أمرك !

٨ - ليلة مباركة !

2 Jaak

Jack

Pronounce : fi th-thaamina wan-nisf (2), min fadlik

English : At half past eight (2) (in the eighth and the half), please.

3 'al khaadim

The valet

Pronounce : tayyib ! wamaadha tufaddil lil-futoor ?

English : Good. And what do you prefer for breakfast ?

4 'al khaadim

The valet

Pronounce : hal tureed qahwa 'am (3) haleeb(an) 'am shaay ?

English : Do you want coffee or (3) milk or tea ?

5 Jaak

Jack

Pronounce : 'a^εtini qahwa bihaleeb (4)

English : Give me coffee with milk (4).

6 Jaak

Jack

Pronounce : ma^εa khubz wazubda wa^εasal

English : With bread and butter and honey.

7 'al khaadim

The valet

Pronounce : tahta 'amrik !

English : Very well, sir (under your order).

8 'al khaadim

The valet

Pronounce : layla mubaaraka.

English : Good (blessed) night.

137

NOTES

1 The word for "tomorrow" is **ghadan** غَدًا . (It is in fact the adverbial form of **ghad,** meaning "the next day".) The word for "the morning" is **'aṣ-ṣabaaḥ,** which, with the adverbial ending -a, means *"in the morning"*. Here we want to combine the two words to say "tomorrow morning" — that is, *"in the morning of to-morrow"* ; and we combine them as follows :

ṣabaaḥa ghadin   صَباحَ غَدٍ

What we have here is a "yoked couple". (If you are not sure that you know exactly what this means, stop whatever you are doing and take another look at page 70.) The -**in** ending of **ghadin** "tomorrow", contains "of". Because the word is yoked to "mor-ning", it automatically makes "morning" *definite,* in grammatical terms ; so the object-adverb case ending used is -a : **ṣabaaḥa.** Furthermore, since it is made definite just by being yoked to **ghadin,** it no longer needs the definite article **'al**, which is there-fore dropped.

The same principle of words acting as yoked couples applies to such other expressions as :

This morning	**ṣabaaḥa l-yawm(i)**	صَباحَ اليَوم
(The morning of today)		
Tomorrow evening	**masaa'a ghad(in)**	مَساءَ غَد
(The evening of tomorrow)		
This evening	**masaa'a l'yawm(i)**	مَساءَ اليَوم
(The evening of today)		

2 The word for "hour" (or "o'clock") is omitted here, as it usually is in English also. See Lesson 4, Note 2.

3 The word for "or" in Arabic is **'aw** أو in a *statement* ("You may have your coffee black or white"), but **'am** أُم in a *question* ("Do you want coffee or milk ?")

4 In Lesson 22, Note 7, we saw some uses of the preposition **bi** بـ , meaning "with", in a certain number of different senses. This preposition is used when we want to say coffee with milk in it (that is, combined with it) :

qahwa biḥaleeb   قَهوة بِحليب

But if we mean coffee *along with* milk (separately), the word for "with" is **ma ᶜa** مَع . In the same way, if we were asking for

138

cheese "with bread", we would say :

ma$^\epsilon$a khubz　　　　　مع خبز

The Arabic word for "without" is *bila* بلا , which is *bi* plus
the negative *la*, "not".

EXERCISES

١- في أيِّ فندق تنزل عادةً ؟

1　fi 'ayyi funduq tanzil $^\epsilon$aadatan ?
　In what hotel do you usually stay ?

٢- هل يريدون شاياً أم حليباً ؟

2　hal yureedoon shaay(an) 'am haleeb(an) ?
　Do they want tea or milk ?

٣- في أيّةِ ساعةٍ يقدّمون
العشاءُ هنا ؟

3　fi 'ayya(ti) saa$^\epsilon$a yuqaddimoona l-$^\epsilon$ashaa'(a) huna ?
　At what time do they serve dinner here ?

في أيّةِ ساعةٍ يُقَدَّمُ العشاءُ هنا ؟

3a　fi 'ayya(ti) saa$^\epsilon$a yuqaddamu l-$^\epsilon$ashaa'(u) huna ?
　At what time is dinner served here ?

٤- في التّاسعةِ بالضّبطِ !

4　fi t-taasi$^\epsilon$a bid-dabt
　At nine o'clock sharp (exactly).

٥- هل تفضّلون أن نقدّمَ لكمُ
الفطور في غرفتكم ؟

5　hal tufaddiloon 'an nuqaddima lakumu l-futoor fi
　ghurfatikum ?
　Do you [plur.] prefer us to (that we) serve you break-
　fast in your [plur.] room ?

139

إلى المطعم

(جاك ينزل مـن غرفتـه ويخرج
مِنَ الفندق)

١ـ سامحني ، يا سيّدي ، هل تعرف
أيـن «مطعمُ الواحة» ؟

٢ـ قريبًا مـن ساحةِ المحكمة ،
في شارع «ابن رشـد »

٣ـ هل هو بعيـد ؟

٤ـ لا ، أبـدًا ؛ خذِ الشّارعَ
الأوّل على اليميـن

The lesson the fifth and the twentieth

Pronounce : 'ila l-mat^ɛam
English : To the restaurant

(Jaak yanzil min ghurfatihi wayakhruj mina l-funduq)
(Jack comes down from his room and goes out of the hotel.)

1 Jaak 'ila 'ahadi l-^ɛaabireen	*Pronounce* : saamihni, ya sayyidi ; hal ta^ɛrif 'ayna mat^ɛamu l-waaha ?
Jack to a passer-by	*English* : Excuse me, sir, do you know where the Oasis Restaurant (is) ?

2 'al ^ɛaabir	*Pronounce* : qareeban min saahati l-mahkama, fi shaari^ɛ 'ibn rushd
The passer-by	*English* : Near Courthouse Square in Ibn Rushd Street.

3 Jaak	*Pronounce* : hal huwa ba^ɛeed ?
Jack	*English* : (Is) it [masc.] far ?

4 'al ^ɛaabir	*Pronounce* : la, 'abadan ; khudhi sh-shaari^ɛa l-'awwal ^ɛala l-yameen
The passer-by	*English* : No, not at all ; take the first street (the street the first) on the right.

141

٥ ـ بعد ذلك ، إقطعْ ساحةَ المحَكمة و دُرْ على اليسار

٦ ـ و هناك تلقى① شارع«ابن رشد»

٧ ـ ممنون !

٨ ـ عفوًا !

★

NOTE

1 There are three things to notice in this phrase, ''And there you will find...'' : wahunaaka talqa و هناك تلقى .
The first is the omission of sa to give a specifically future sense to the verb in the pending aspect [See Lesson 16, Note 1] : the future sense is clear enough without it.

The second is the verb used for ''you find'', talqa تلقى . This in fact means ''you meet'' or ''you come upon'' ; it is derived from the same root as the word for ''meeting'' or ''encounter'', liqaa' لقاء .
The third is a matter of word-formation. The complete basic consonant root from which both **talqa** and **liqaa'** are derived is **l-q-y**. Then where is the **y** ? You will remember that **y** is a *semi*-consonant ; like **'alif** (a) and **w**, it serves also as a vowel. When the last consonant of a root is such a *semi*-consonant, one of three things may happen to it in the words to which it gives rise :

(a) It may disappear entirely.
(b) It may change to a hamza, as it does in **liqaa'**.
(c) It may change to one of its two sister semi-consonants.
In **talqa**, it changes to **'alif**. (In this instance, which occurs at the end of a word, a shortened **'alif** is used, called **'alif maqsoora**. You can see it change to a normal **'alif** in Sentence 4 of the Exercise below.)

142

5 'al ^εaabir   *Pronounce* : ba^εda dhaalik, 'iqta^ε saahata
l-mahkama wadur ^εala l-yasaar
The passer-by   *English* : Then (after that) cross (cut)
Courthouse Square and turn left.

6 'al ^εaabir   *Pronounce* : wahunaaka talqa (1) shaari^ε
'ibn rushd
The passer-by   *English* : And there you will find (1)
Ibn Rushd Street.

7 Jaak   *Pronounce* : mamnoon !
Jack   *English* : (Much) obliged.

8 'al ^εaabir   *Pronounce* : ^εafwan
The passer-by   *English* : Don't mention it.

★

EXERCISES

١- في أيِّ شارع يوجد فندقُ المحطّةِ ؟

1 fi 'ayyi shaari^ε yoojad funduqu l-mahatta ?
In what street is the railway (station) hotel ?

٢- أنزل في فندقِ المطارِ؛ وأنتَ ،
أيـن تنزل عادةً ؟

2 'anzil fi funduqi l-mataar, wa'anta, 'ayna tanzil ^εaada-tan ?
I stay at the airport hotel ; and you, where do you generally stay ?

143

٣- في الشّارع الرّابع على اليسار،
قبل السّاحة

3 fi sh-shaari‘i r-raabi‘ ‘ala l-yasaar, qabla s-saaha
In the fourth street on the left, before the square.

٤- ستلقاهُ بسهولة

4 satalqaahu bisuhoola
You will find it easily (with ease).

خذ الشّارع الأوّل
إلى اليمين

الدّرسُ السّادس و العشرون

’ad-darsu s-saadis wal- ‘ishroon

في المطعم

(جاك يصل إلى المطعم و يدخل)

١- السّلامُ عليكم ⓢ !

144

GRAMMAR : Verbs

The **indicative**, in the **pending aspect**, of two more verbs, (singular only).

MEET (laqiya) (in the sense of "encounter" or "find" or "come on") **(Root : L-Q-Y)**

I meet	'alqa	أَلْقَى
You [masc.] meet	talqa	تَلْقَى
You [fem.] meet	talqayna	تَلْقَيْنَ
He meets	yalqa	يَلْقَى

CUT (qata$^\epsilon$a) (Root : Q-T-E)

I cut	'aqta$^\epsilon$u	أَقْطَع
You [masc.] cut	taqta$^\epsilon$u	تَقْطَع
You [fem.] cut	taqta$^\epsilon$eena	تَقْطَعِين
He cuts	yaqta$^\epsilon$u	يَقْطَع
Cut ! [masc. sing. imperative]	'iqta$^\epsilon$	إِقْطَعْ !

Lesson 26

The lesson the sixth and the twentieth

Pronounce : fi l-mat$^\epsilon$am
English : In the restaurant

Pronounce : (Jaak yaṣil 'ila l-mat$^\epsilon$am wayadkhul)
English : (Jack arrives at (to) the restaurant and goes in.)

1 Jaak 'ila   *Pronounce* : 'as-salaam(u) $^\epsilon$alaykum (1)
   l-gharsoon
   Jack to the   *English* : Good evening (1).
   waiter

145

٢- و عليكمُ السّلامُ ①

٣- أُريد أن أتعشّى

٤- طيّب ، يا سيّدي ؛ هل أنت
وحدَك ؟

٥- نعم

٦- هل تريد أن نجلسَ إلى
هذه المائدة ؟

٧- أم تفضّل أن تأكلَ ②

في الطّابقِ الأوّل ④

٨- أفضّل أن أصعدَ إلى
الطّابقِ الأوّل

146

2 'al gharsoon
The waiter

Pronounce : wa^εalaykumu s-salaam (1)
English : Good evening (1).

3 Jaak
Jack

Pronounce : 'ureed 'an 'ata^εashsha
English : I'd like to have dinner.

4 'al gharsoon

The waiter

Pronounce : ṭayyib ya sayyidi ; hal 'anta
waḥdak ?
English : Very good, sir ; are you alone ?

5 Jaak
Jack

Pronounce : na^εam
English : Yes.

6 'al gharsoon

The waiter

Pronounce : hal tureed 'an tajlisa 'ila
haadhihi l-maa'ida ?
English : Would you like to sit at this
table ?

7 'al gharsoon

The waiter

Pronounce : 'am tufaddil 'an ta'kula
(2) fi t-ṭaabiqi l-'awwal (3) ?
English : Or do you prefer to (that
you) eat (2) on the first floor (3) ?

8 Jaak

Jack

Pronounce : 'ufaddil 'an 'as^εada 'ila
t-ṭaabiqi l-'awwal
English : I prefer to (that I) go up to the
first floor.

٩- فوقَ ، ستأكل
في جوٍّ هادىٍٔ

١٠- هناكَ قليلٌ مِنَ④ النّاس
و مِنَ الضّجيج

١١- اِتبعني ، مِن فضلكَ ... هل
أنتَ هنا منذ زمنٍ طويل ؟

١٢- لا ، وصلتُ مساءَ اليوم
مِنْ باريس

١٣- أهلاً بك !

٭

NOTES

1 The everyday greeting, 'as-salaam(u) $^\epsilon$alaykum is a form of
"hello" used at any time of day or night. The customary reply
to it is the same phrase inverted : wa$^\epsilon$alaykumu s-salaam. (Notice
the use here of u as a bridging vowel.) There are more specific
forms of greeting for specific times of day. For example :

9 'al gharsoon   *Pronounce* : fawqa, sata'kul fi jaw(win) haadi'

The waiter   *English* : Upstairs (above), you will eat in a quiet atmosphere.

10 'al gharsoon   *Pronounce* : hunaaka qaleel mina (4) n-naas wamina d-dajeej

The waiter   *English* : There (are) not many (4) people and (there is) not much noise.

11 'al gharsoon   *Pronounce* : 'itba$^\epsilon$ni, min fadlik... hal 'anta huna mundhu zaman taweel ?

The waiter   *English* : Follow me, please... Have you been here long (you here since a long time) ?

12 Jaak   *Pronounce* : la, wasaltu masa'a l-yawm min baarees

Jack   *English* : No, I arrived from Paris this evening.

13 'al gharsoon   *Pronounce* : 'ahlan bik

The waiter   *English* : Welcome.

✳

(a) Good morning   sabaaha l-khayr   صباحَ الخير
     (Morning of goodness)

The usual reply to this is :
Good morning   sabaaha n-noor   صباحَ النّور
     (Morning of light)

(b) Good evening   masaa'a l-khayr   مساءَ الخير
     (Evening of goodness)

149

2 The Arabic verbs for "eat" (**'akala** = he ate) and for "take" (**'akhadha** = he took), which we saw earlier, have in common a similarity of structure which should here be noted. That is, the first consonant in the root of both verbs is a **hamza**. This **hamza** is dropped when the verb is put in the imperative.
Thus :

You take	ta'khudh	تَأْخُذ
Take ! [masc.]	khudh !	خُذْ !
You eat	ta'kul	تَأْكُل
Eat ! [masc.]	kul !	كُلْ !

3

"First" [masc.] is	'awwal	أَوّل
"First" [fem.] is	'oola	أُولى
"Last" [masc.] is	'akheer	أَخِير
"Last" [fem.] is	'akheera	أَخِيرة

4 The Arabic here means literally, "There (are) few in the way of people and little in the way of noise" ; the expression "few in the way of" is rendered by **qaleel min**. We have already encountered this turn of phrase. The same idea could also be expressed as, "There (are) people few and noise little" : **hunaaka naas qaleeloon wadajeej qaleel**. In the first instance, the words "few" and "little" are nouns denoting a small number or quantity ; in the second instance they are adjectives modifying the nouns "people" and "noise".

EXERCISES

١ـ سَتَرَوْنَ : الطَّعام لَذيذ و الجوّ هادِئ ٴ

1 satarawna : 'at-ta^caam ladheedh wal- jaw w haadi' !
You [plur.] will see : the food is excellent and the atmosphere is quiet.

150

٢ـ كم أُنتـم ؟

2 kam 'antum ?
How many are you ?

٣ـ سأجلس هنا ؛ أنا تعبان وجوعان

3 sa'ajlis huna ; 'ana ta$^\epsilon$baan wajaw$^\epsilon$aan
I'll sit here ; I (am) tired and hungry.

٤ـ هل أنتِ عطشانة ؟ هل تريدين
قليلٌ منَ الماء ؟

4 hal 'anti $^\epsilon$aṭshaana ? hal tureedeen qaleel(an) mina
l-maa' ?
Are you [fem.] thirsty ? Do you [fem.] want a little
water ?

٥ـ لا، شكراً ؛ أنا غير عطشانة
ولكنيّ جوعانة ، أُريد أن آكل

5 la, shukran ; 'ana ghayr $^\epsilon$aṭshaana walaakinni jaw$^\epsilon$aana ;
'ureed 'an 'aakula
No, thank you ; I (am) not thirsty but I (am) hungry ;
I'd like to eat.

٦ـ منذ كم وصلتُ ؟

6 mundhu kam waṣalat ?
How long ago did she arrive ?

151

٧- هي هنا منذ زمن طويل ؛ ولكنّها
لا تعرفُ المدينة جيّدًا

7 hiya huna mundhu zaman ṭaweel ; walaakinnaha la
taᶜrifᵢ l-madeena jayyidan
She has been here for a long time ; but she doesn't
know the city well.

GRAMMAR : Verbs

The **indicative**, in the **pending aspect**, of another four verbs (singular only).

EAT ('akala) (Root : '-K-L)

I eat	'aakulu	آكل
You [masc.] eat	ta'kulu	تأكل
You [fem.] eat	ta'kuleena	تأكلين
He eats	ya'kulu	يأكل
Eat ! [imperative, masc. sing.]	kul	كل !

SIT DOWN (jalasa) (Root : J-L-S)

I sit down	'ajlisu	أجلس
You [masc.] sit down	tajlisu	تجلس
You [fem.] sit down	tajliseena	تجلسين
He sits down	yajlisu	يجلس
Sit down ! [imperative, masc. sing.]	'ijlis	إجلس !

152

GO UP or COME UP (sa$^\epsilon$ida) (Root : S$_\bullet$-$^\epsilon$-D)

I go up	'as$^\epsilon$adu	أصعد
You [masc.] go up	tas$^\epsilon$adu	تصعد
You [fem.] go up	tas$^\epsilon$adeena	تصعدين
He goes up	yas$^\epsilon$adu	يصعد
Go up ! [imperative, masc. sing.]	'is$^\epsilon$ad	اصعد !

COME IN or GO IN or ENTER (dakhala) (Root : D-KH-L)

I come in	'adkhulu	أدخل
You [masc.] come in	tadkhulu	تدخل
You [fem.] come in	tadkhuleena	تدخلين
He comes in	yadkhulu	يدخل
Come in ! [imperative, masc. sing.]	'udkhul	أدخل !

153

في المطعم

١- سأجلس هناكَ ، قربَ النَّافذة ①

٢- كما تريد

٣- ماذا¹ تأكل ؟

٤- هل عندكم (وجبات) ⑤

شرقيَّة ؟

٥- (بالطَّبع) ، يا سيِّدي ؛ ها هي

القائمة ؛ تفضَّل !

(جاك ينظر في ② القائمة)

154

The lesson the seventh and the twentieth

Pronounce : fi l-mat‌ᵉam

English : In the restaurant

1 Jaak   *Pronounce* : sa'ajlis hunaaka, qurba (1) n-naafidha

Jack   *English* : I'll sit here, near (1) the window.

2 'al gharsoon   *Pronounce* : kama tureed

The waiter   *English* : As you wish.

3 'al gharsoon   *Pronounce* : maadha ta'kul ?

The waiter   *English* : What will you (have to) eat ?

4 Jaak   *Pronounce* : hal ᵉindakum wajbaat (2) sharqiyya ?

Jack   *English* : Have you any Middle Eastern dishes (2) ?

5 'al gharsoon   *Pronounce* : bit-tabᵉ, ya sayyidi ; ha hiya l-qaa'ima ; tafaddal

The waiter   *English* : Of course, sir ; here is the menu ; take your time.

(Jaak yanzur fi (3) l-qaa'ima)

(Jack studies (examines) (3) the menu.)

155

٦- أعطني كبابًا مع رزّ

٧- ماذا تأخذ في الأوّل ؟

٨- لا شيء ، لست جوعان ④
جدًّا ، ولكنّي عطشان

٩- ماذا تريد أن تشربَ ؟

١٠- هل عندكم خمرٌ جيّدٌ ؟

١١- نعم ، عندنا خمرٌ
من الدّرجةِ الأولى

6 Jaak
Jack

Pronounce : 'a^ϵtini kabaab(an) ma^ϵa ruzz
English : Give me a shish kebab with rice.

7 'al gharsoon
The waiter

Pronounce : maadha ta'khudh fi l-'awwal?
English : What will you have as a first course ?

كُتـشـمْ

8 Jaak

Jack

Pronounce : la shay'; lastu jaw^ϵaan (4) jiddan, walaakinni ^ϵatshaan
English : Nothing ; I (am) not very hungry (4), but I (am) thirsty.

9 'al gharsoon
The waiter

Pronounce : maadha tureed 'an tashraba ?
English : What would you like to drink ?

10 Jaak

Jack

Pronounce : hal ^ϵindakum khamr(un) jayyid ?
English : Have you a good wine ?

11 'al gharsoon

The waiter

Pronounce : na^ϵam, ^ϵindana khamr(un) mina d-darajati l-'oola
English : Yes, we have a first-rate wine.

NOTES

1 The preposition **qurba** قُرْبَ , "near", is more or less interchangeable with the expression **qareeban min** قَرِيبًا مِنْ , "close to" (literally : "neighbouring from"). It is in fact the noun **qurb(un)**, "nearness", with the ending -a of a definite noun in the object/adverb case. Many Arabic prepositions are similarly nouns "frozen" in the object/adverb case with the definite ending -a. Others of this sort that you will encounter include :

under	**taḥta**	تَحْتَ
above	**fawqa**	فَوْقَ
before	**qabla**	قَبْلَ
after	**ba͏ᵉda**	بَعْدَ

2 The singular form of this plural, **wajbaat** وَجَبَات , meaning "dishes" (things to eat, not tableware), is **wajba** وَجْبَة . Because it is **a plural of an inanimate thing**, its adjective is in the **feminine singular** [See Lessons 9 and 14]. Here are a few more examples of this principle :

A beautiful car [fem.]	**sayyaara jameela**	سَيَّارَة جَمِيلَة
Beautiful cars	**sayyaaraat jameela**	سَيَّارَات جَمِيلَة
A large office [masc.]	**maktab kabeer**	مَكْتَب كَبِير
Large offices	**makaatib kabeera**	مَكَاتِب كَبِيرَة

3 We will see in Lesson 31 how to conjugate the verb "look" (**naẓara** = he looked). As in English, this verb is given different shades of meaning by the preposition that is used with it, which may be **'ila** إِلَى ("at", "towards") or **fi** فِي ("into") :

He looks at (or towards) the window   **yanẓur 'ila n-naafidha**

يَنْظُر إِلَى النَّافِذَة

He looks into (i.e. examines or scrutinizes) the police form.   **yanẓur fi waraqati sh-shurṭa**

يَنْظُر فِي وَرَقَةِ الشُّرْطَة

158

4 We have already seen (in Lessons 8 and 14) that the Arabic verbs meaning "to be" and "not to be" are regarded as active (transitive) verbs, and that the predicates which follow them therefore behave like direct objects of these verbs, with the object-case endings (-a for definite words, -an for indefinite words). Here, the predicate or direct object of the verb "not to be", **laysa**, is the indefinite adjective "hungry" — which we should therefore expect to be written **jaw$^\epsilon$aanan**. But we see that it is in fact written **jaw$^\epsilon$aan**. Why ?

You will remember that, on page 102, we made the acquaintance of some common adjectives describing **states or conditions** of body or mind whose vowel pattern is made up of **a** plus **aan**, as in **jaw$^\epsilon$aan**. To the same grammatical group belong a number of other adjectives whose usual pattern is **'a** plus **a**, as in **'aṭrash** ("deaf"), and which denote **infirmities** : blind, deaf, dumb, etc. This group also includes adjectives of **color** [See Lesson 9] as well as **comparatives** and **superlatives**.

What is peculiar about this group is that the words in it do not conform to the normal rules for case endings — that is, -u, -a and -i for definite words, -un, -an and -in for indefinite words. Instead, when they are *indefinite,* they take the case endings for definite words (without "n"), and only two rather than three of them : -u in the subject case, -a in both the object and the oblique cases.

In practice — that is, in the everyday spoken language — these endings are not pronounced at all unless they are needed for "bridging". Hence **jaw$^\epsilon$aan** rather than **jaw$^\epsilon$aana** ; and, similarly, **$^\epsilon$aṭshaan** ("thirsty") rather than **$^\epsilon$aṭshaana**.

One other point is worth mentioning here : Instead of using the verb "not to be" to say "I am not hungry" — **lastu jaw$^\epsilon$aan** لست جوعان , we could use the noun phrase, "I (am) other than hungry" — **'ana ghayr jaw$^\epsilon$aan** أنا غير جوعان [See Lesson 23]. We will come back to the matter of negative statements in Lesson 35.

EXERCISES in the use of the verb "not to be"

لست هنا منذ زمن طويل ـ١

1 **lastu** huna mundhu zaman taweel
I have not been here long (I am not here since a long time).

لست تعبان ـ٢

2 **lasta** ta‘baan
You [masc. sing] are not tired.

لست فرحانة ؟ ـ٣

3 **lasti** farhaana ?
You [fem. sing.] are not pleased ?

ليس موجودًا ـ٤

4 **laysa** mawjoodan
He is not here.

ليست معنا ـ٥

5 **laysat** ma‘ana
She is not with us.

لسنا مسلمين ـ٦

6 **lasna** muslimeen(a)
We are not Moslems.

لستم قادمين منَ المطار ـ٧

7 **lastum** qaadimeen mina l-mataar
You are not coming from the airport.

ليسوا جالسين قربَ الباب ـ٨

8 **laysu** jaaliseen qurba l-baab
They are not sitting near the door.

MORE EXERCISES, this time in **the use of the espression "ghayr"** غَيْر ("other than"), preceded by the personal subject pronoun [See Lesson 6], in place of "not to be".

1 **'anta** ghayr ta⁶baan
   You [masc. sing.] are not tired.
   (You other than tired.)

١- أُنْتَ غَيْرِ تَعْبان

2 **'anti** ghayr saa'iḥa
   You [fem. sing.] are not (a) tourist.
   (You other than tourist.)

٢- أُنْتِ غَيْرِ سائِحَة.

3 **huwa** ghayr mawjood
   He is not here.
   (He other than here.)

٣- هُوَ غَيْرِ مَوْجُود

4 **naḥnu** ghayr ṣaḥafiyyeen(a)
   We are not journalists.
   (We other than journalists.)

٤- نَحْنُ غَيْرِ صَحَفِيِّيِن

5 **'antum** ghayr muslimeen(a)
   You are not Moslems.
   (You other than Moslems.)

٥- أُنْتُمْ غَيْرِ مُسْلِمِين

6 **hum** ghayr qaadimeen mina l-funduq
   They are not coming from the hotel.
   (They other than coming from the hotel.)

٦- هُمْ غَيْرِ قادِمِين مِنَ الفُنْدُق

مَاذَا تَأْخُذُ فِي الأَوَّلِ ؟

مُراجَعة.

١-

هل يمكن أن أُدَخِّنَ ؟

٢-

أَتَمَنَّى لك سفرًا طيِّبًا

٣-

في أيَّةِ ساعةٍ تصلُ الطَّائرةُ ؟

٤-

ستصلُ الطَّائرةُ بعد خمسِ دقائق فقط

The lesson the eight and the twentieth.

Pronounce : muraaja$^\epsilon$a
English : Review

We will devote this fourth review lesson almost entirely to forming sentences based on what you have learned up to now. You will see at once that you have come a long way in a relatively short time. We suggest that you repeat these sentences aloud over and over until they sink in. Try to do so without looking either at the transcriptions or at the English translations.

1 hal yumkin 'an 'udakhkhina ?
May (is it possible that) I smoke ?

2 'atamanna lak safar (an) ṭayyib(an)
I wish you a good trip.

3 fi 'ayya(ti) saa$^\epsilon$a taṣilu ṭ-ṭaa'ira ?
At what time does the plane arrive ?

4 sataṣilu ṭ-ṭaa'ira ba$^\epsilon$da khams daqaa'iq faqaṭ
The plane will arrive in a mere ten minutes (in ten minutes only).

163

٥-

ما هي مهنتُكَ ؟

٦-

أعرف إسمَهُ ولكن ، ما أعطاني
عنوانَهُ

٧-

هل ترى حقيبتَهُ ؟ هي هذه السّوداء

٨-

وها هي حقيبتي : هذه البيضاء

٩-

وصلت زوجتُهُ معَهُ بالطّائرة
مساءَ أمس

١٠-

سأعطيك جوازي وسأفتح
أمتعتي

5   ma hiya mihnatuk ?
What is your profession ?

6   'a^εrifu smahu walaakin, ma 'a^εtaani ^εunwaanahu.
I know his name, but he didn't give me his address.

7   hal tara haqeebatahu ? hiya haadhihi s-sawdaa'
Do you [masc. sing.] see his suitcase ? It is this black one.

8   waha hiya haqeebati : haadhihi l-baydaa'
And here is my suitcase : this white one.

9   wasalat zawjatuh(u) ma^εahu bit-taa'ira, masaa'a 'ams
His wife arrived with him yesterday evening.

10   sa'u^εteek jawaazi wasa'aftah 'amti^εati
I'll give you my passport and I'll open my baggage.

١١ -
هل مكتب تغييرِ النُّقود مفتوح
مساءً اليوم ؟
١٢ -
ليست معي نقود عربيّة كثيرة
ليس معي كثيرٌ منَ النُّقودِ العربيّة
١٣ -
إلى أينَ تريد أن أذهبَ ؟
١٤ -
هناكَ موقف تاكسي أمامَ بابِ الفندق
يوجد موقف تاكسي أمامَ بابِ الفندق
١٥ -
تعلَّمت العربيّة أنا وحدي
١٦ -
أنا عطشان ؛ هل يمكن أن أشربَ
كأس ماءٍ باردٍ ؟

166

11   hal maktab taghyeeri n-nuqood maftooḥ masaa'a
l-yawm ?
Is the exchange office open this evening ?

12   laysat ma^عi nuqood ^عarabiyya katheera
                        or
laysa ma^عi katheer mina n-nuqoodi l-^عarabiyya
I haven't much Arab money.

13   'ila 'ayna tureed 'an 'adhhaba ?
Where do you want me to go ?

14   hunaak(a) [*or* yoojad] mawqif taaksi 'amaama baabi
l-funduq
There is a taxi station in front of the hotel door.

15   ta^عallamtu l-^عarabiyya 'ana waḥdi
I learned Arabic by myself.

16   'ana ^عatshaan ; hal yumkin 'an 'ashraba ka's maa'
baarid ?
I [masc.] (am) thirsty ; may (is it possible that) I
drink a glass of cold water ?

هو في مكتبهِ دائمًا ، منَ الثّامنة
صباحًا حتّى السّادسة مساءً

GRAMMAR : Plurals

While some Arabic plurals are formed, as in English, just by adding
endings to the singular words, most are formed by **internal changes**
within the words. These are called "internal" or "broken" plurals.
The changes follow no fixed rules, but they generally conform to
a few standard "models". So as to familiarize you with them, we
give you below, grouped by "models", a short list of singular and
plural forms of words used in this book. We show in bold-face
capitals the framework of consonant roots (3 or 4) around which
the changes are made.

English	Singular	Plural
Lesson	DaRS	DuRooS
Glass	Ka'S	Ku'ooS
Plate	SaHN	SuHooN
Flower	ZaHR	ZuHooR
Newspaper	JaReeDa	JaRaa'iD
Suitcase	HaQeeBa	HaQaa'iB
Minute	DaQeeQa	DaQaa'iQ

17 huwa fi maktabih(i) daa'iman, mina th-thaamina
sabaahan hatta s-saadisa masaa'an
He is always in his office from eight in the morning
to six in the evening.

English	Singular	Plural
Hotel	FuNDuQ	FaNaaDiQ
Seat	MaQ^εaD	MaQaa^εiD
Office	MaKTaB	MaKaaTiB
Child	WaLaD	'aWLaaD
Trip	SaFaR	'aSFaaR
Number	RaQM	'aRQaaM
Quarter	RuB^ε	'aRBaa^ε
Half	NiSF	'aNSaaF
Tenth	^εuSHR	'a^εSHaaR
Key	MiFTaaH	MaFaaTeeH
Knife	SiKKeeN	SaKaaKeeN
Orchard	BuSTaaN	BaSaaTeeN
Street	SHaaRi^ε	SHawaaRi^ε
Floor	TaaBiQ	TawaaBiQ
Room	GHuRFa	GHuRaF
Box	^εuLBa	^εuLaB
Country	BaLaD	BiLaaD
Town	MaDeeNa	MuDuN

الدَّرسُ التّاسع و العشرون

'ad-darsu t-taasi$^\epsilon$ wal-$^\epsilon$ishroon

في المطعم

(جاك يسمع أغنية عربية)

١ـ هذه الأُغنية جميلة !

٢ـ هل تحبُّ الموسيقى العربيّة ؟

٣ـ نعم ، جدّاً ... وكذلك أُحبُّ (١) الطَّعامُ العربيّ

٤ـ ألحمدُ لِلَّه (٢) !

(يرجعُ الغرسون)

170

The lesson the ninth and the twentieth

Pronounce : fi l-mat$^\epsilon$am
English : In the restaurant

(Jaak yasma$^\epsilon$ 'ughniya $^\epsilon$arabiyya)
(Jack hears an Arabic song.)

1	Jaak Jack	*Pronounce* : haadhihi l-'ughniya jameela *English* : This song (is) lovely.

2	'al gharsoon The waiter	*Pronounce* : hal tuḥibbu l-mooseeqa l-$^\epsilon$arabiyya ? *English* : Do you like Arabic music ?

3	Jaak Jack	*Pronounce :* na$^\epsilon$am, jiddan... wakadhaalik (1) 'uḥibbu ṭ-ṭa$^\epsilon$aama l-$^\epsilon$arabi(yya) *English* : Yes, very much... I also (1) like Arabic food.

4	'al gharsoon The waiter	*Pronounce* : 'al-ḥamdu li-llaah ! (2) *English* : Fine ! (God be praised !) (2)

(yarji$^\epsilon$u l-gharsoon)
(The waiter [goes to the kitchen and] comes back.)

٥ـ تفضّل، يا سيّدي : هذا هو
الكباب ، و هذا هو الرّزّ! هنيئًا

٦ـ شكرًا ! ولكن ، نسيت
الخبز

٧ـ عفوًا ؛ أُحضرهُ حالًّا

٨ـ لا يهمّ

(يعودُ الغرسون مرّةً أُخرى)

٩ـ هاهو الخبز و هاهو الخمر

١٠ـ متشكّر [٣] ! كأنّي [٤]
في الجنّة !

172

5 'al gharsoon   *Pronounce* : tafaddal, ya sayyidi :
haadha huwa l-kabaab wahaadha huwa
r-ruzz. hanee'an !

   The waiter   *English* : Here you are, sir ; here is the
shish kebab and here is the rice.
Enjoy your meal (Good appetite) !

6 Jaak   *Pronounce* : shukran ! walaakin,
naseeta l-khubz

   Jack   *English* : Thank you !... But you have
forgotten the bread.

7 'al gharsoon   *Pronounce* : ᵉafwan, 'uhdiruhu haalan

   The waiter   *English* : Sorry, I'll bring it at once.

8 Jaak   *Pronounce* : la yuhimm

   Jack   *English* : No matter.

(yaᵉoodu l-gharsoon marratan 'ukhra)
(The waiter comes back again.)

9 'al gharsoon   *Pronounce* : ha huwa l-khubz waha
huwa l-khamr

   The waiter   *English* : Here is the bread and here
is the wine.

10 Jaak   *Pronounce*: mutashakkir (3), ka'anni(4)
fi l-janna !

   Jack   *English* : Thank you (3). It's out
of this world (as if (4) I (were) in
Paradise) !

NOTES

1 Jiddan جِدّاً in fact means "very". It is used here in the sense of "very much". As for **kadhaalik** كَذلِك , which we are meeting here for the first time, it is made up of **ka** ("like") and **dhaalik** ("that"), and can be variously translated as "likewise", "similarly", "in addition", "also". It is more or less synonymous with **'aydan** أَيضاً

2 The commonly used expression, **'al-ḥamdu li-llaah** أَلحَمدُ لِلّه which literally means "God be praised", can be translated in many ways. It expresses pleasure, approbation, relief and the like. We have seen it before in Lesson 6, Sentence 3.

3 This is still another way of saying "Thank you". It consists of the participle **mutashakkir** مُتَشَكِّر whose literal sense is "thanking". The ways of saying thanks that we have seen before are :

shukran	شُكراً	The everyday "thank you"
shukran jazeelan	شُكراً جَزيلٌ	"Thank you very much"
'alf shukr	أَلف شُكر	"A thousand thanks"
'ashkuruk	أَشكُرك	"I thank you"
mamnoon	مَمنون	"Much obliged"

4 As you see from our translation, the turn of phrase here is not more (or less) extravagant in Arabic than in English. But we want to call your attention to the curious way in which Arabic uses the word for "as if", **ka'anna** كَأَنَّ . Like the word for "but", **laakinna** لكِنَّ it must *either* be followed directly by a noun in the object case (*"As if a camel* were a household pet"), *or* have attached to it as an ending one of the object pronouns, **me, you, him**, etc. We thus obtain :

174

As if I (to me)	ka'anni or ka'annani	كَأَنِّي ـ كَأَنَّنِي
As if (to) you [masc.]...	ka'annaka	كَأَنَّكَ
As if (to) you [fem.]	ka'annaki	كَأَنَّكِ
As if he (to him)...	ka'annahu	كَأَنَّهُ
As if she (to her)...	ka'annaha	كَأَنَّهَا
As if we (to us)...	ka'annana or ka'anna	كَأَنَّنَا ـ كَأَنَّا
As if (to) you...	ka'annakum	كَأَنَّكُم
As if they (to them)...	ka'annahum	كَأَنَّهُم

EXERCISES

١ـ تَتَكَلَّمُ العَرَبِيَّةَ كَأَنَّكَ عَرَبِيّ

1 tatakallamu l-ᵉarabiyya ka'annaka ᵉarabi(yyun)
You [masc. sing.] speak Arabic as if you (were) an Arab.

٢ـ كَأَنَّا فِي بَلَدِنَا

2 ka'annana fi baladina
(It is) as if we were in our (own) country.

٣ـ نَسِيتُ اِسمَهُ وَكَذَلِكَ عُنوانَهُ

3 naseetu smahu wakadhaalik ᵉunwaanah(u)
I have forgotten his name as well as his address.

٤ـ هَل تُحِبّونَ الكَباب بِالرُّزِّ ؟

4 hal tuḥibboona l-kabaab bir-ruzz ?
Do you [plur.] like shish kebab with rice ?

GRAMMAR : Verbs

The **pending aspect** (indicative, singular) of **LOVE** or **LIKE** ('aḥabba), (Root : Ḥ-B-B)

I love	'uḥibbu	أُحِبّ
You [masc.] love	tuḥibbu	تُحِبّ
You [fem.] love	tuḥibbeena	تُحِبّينَ
He loves	yuḥibbu	يُحِبّ
She loves	tuḥibbu	تُحِبّ

The **completed aspect** of **FORGET** (nasiya) (Root : N-S-Y)

I forgot (or have forgotten)	naseetu	نَسيت
You [masc.] forgot	naseeta	نَسيت
You [fem.] forgot	naseeti	نَسيتِ
He forgot	nasiya	نَسِي
She forgot	nasiyat	نَسيت

الدَّرسُ الثَّلاثُون

'ad-darsu th-thalaathoon

في المطعم

١- مِن فضلك ! أعطني

ملحًا و فلفلًا

176

The **pending aspect** (indicative, singular) of **HEAR** (sami$^\epsilon$a)
(Root : S-M-$^\epsilon$)

I hear	'asma$^\epsilon$u	أسمع
You [masc.] hear	tasma$^\epsilon$u	تسمع
You [fem.] hear	tasma$^\epsilon$eena	تسمعين
He hears	yasma$^\epsilon$u	يسمع
She hears	tasma$^\epsilon$u	تسمع

هنيئاً !

Lesson 30

The lesson the thirtieth

Pronounce : fi l-mat$^\epsilon$am
English : In the restaurant

1 Jaak 'ila   *Pronounce* : min faḍlik ! 'a$^\epsilon$tini milḥ(an)
l'-gharsoon   wafulful(an)
Jack to   *English* : Please ! Give me (some) salt
the waiter   and pepper.

177

٢- طيّب! هل تريد «هريسة»① أيضًا؟

٣- نعم، أحبُّ الطّعامَ الحارَّ ©

(حِباك قد انتهى من أكلِ ما في صحنِهِ)③

٤- اللّه④! أكلت جيّدًا! هذا الطّعام قد فتح شهيّتي

٥- أعطني سلطة طماطم

٦- حباك: وسأعطيك صحنًا آخر، مع سكّين وشوكة أخرى⑤

2 'al gharsoon   *Pronounce* : tayyib. hal tureed "hareesa"
(1) 'aydan ?
   The waiter   *English* : Certainly. Would you also like
(some) "hareesa" (1) ?

3 Jaak   *Pronounce* : na$^\epsilon$am, 'uhibbu t-ta$^\epsilon$aama
l-haarr (2)
   Jack   *English* : Yes, I like spicy (2) food.

(Jaak qadi ntaha min 'akl(i) (3) ma fi sahnihi)
(Jack has finished eating (3) what is in his plate.)

4 Jaak   *Pronounce* : 'allaah (4) ! 'akaltu jayyidan!
haadha t-ta$^\epsilon$aam qad fataha shahiyyati
   Jack   *English* : Lord (4), what a meal (I have
eaten well) ! This food has given me an
appetite (has opened my appetite).

5 Jaak   *Pronounce* : 'a$^\epsilon$tini salata(t) tamaatim
   Jack   *English* : Give me a tomato salad.

6 'al gharsoon   *Pronounce* : haalan : wasa'u$^\epsilon$teeka
sahn(an) 'aakhar, ma$^\epsilon$a sikkeen washawka
'ukhra (5)
   The waiter   *English* : Right away. I'll give you another
plate, with a knife and another fork (5).

179

٧ ـ لا ، لا يهمّ ، ولكن ، أعطني

قارورة ماء

٨ ـ أحضرُها فوراً ، مع السّلطة.

(يعودُ الغرسون مع قارورةِ الماء

وسلطةِ الطّماطم)

٩ ـ هذا هو الماء وها هي السّلطة ،

مع الزّيتِ والخلّ

١٠ ـ شكراً جزيلٌ

NOTES

1 **hareesa** is a hot sauce made of ground-up red peppers.

2 **haarr** حارّ is the word for "hot", used here in the sense of "peppery".

7 Jaak *Pronounce* : la, la yuhimm ; walaakin
'a$^\epsilon$tini qaaroora(t) maa'

  Jack *English* : No, no matter ; but give me a
carafe of water.

8 'al gharsoon *Pronounce* : 'uhdiruha fawran ma$^\epsilon$a
s-salata

  The waiter *English* : I'll bring it immediately
with the salad.

(ya$^\epsilon$oodu l-gharsoon ma$^\epsilon$a qaaroorati l-maa' wasalata(ti)
t-tamaatim)
(The waiter comes back with the carafe of water and the
tomato salad.)

9 'al gharsoon *Pronounce* : haadha huwa l-maa'
waha hiya s-salata, ma$^\epsilon$a z-zayt(i) wal-
khall

  The waiter *English* : This is (it) the water and here
is the salad, with (the) oil and (the)
vinegar.

10 Jaak *Pronounce* : shukran jazeelan

  Jack *English* : Thank you very much.

3 The word "eating", 'akl أَكل is what is called in Arabic a
verbal noun (in English, a gerund, as in **"the pounding** of artillery"
or "**the shooting** of John Dillinger"). The verbal noun 'al 'akl الدُّكل
has the same root as the verb 'akala أَكَلَ , "he ate".

181

We have already seen in earlier lessons a number of other such verbal nouns (or gerunds), which are no less common in Arabic than in English ; and we will see many more. We will also have much more to say later about the way in which various words and word-forms are derived in Arabic from a basic root. (See Introduction, page XL.) Here are some examples, from earlier lessons, of gerunds and verbs derived from the same root :

Verbal Noun			Verb		
'at-tadkheen	التَّدخِين	smoking	dakhkhana	دَخَّنَ	he smoked
'iqaama	إقامة	residing, staying	'aqaama	أَقَامَ	he stayed
'at-taghyeer	التَّغيِير	changing	ghayyara	غَيَّرَ	he changed

4 The name of the Lord is invoked as commonly in Arabic as in English to express pleasure, admiration, astonishment, etc. "Lord, what a meal !" "My God, what a sight !"

5 It may be |unnecessary| by now — but it won't do any harm — to call your attention to the fact that "another plate" and "another fork" become in Arabic "a plate another" and "a fork another". But notice the masculine and feminine forms of the adjective "another".

EXERCISES

١- هل يوجد ملح و فلفل في هذه الوجبة؟

1 Is there (any) salt and pepper in this dish ?

٢- معلوم؛ هذا الطّعام حارٌّ جدًّا

2 Of course ; this food is very spicy.

٣- هل تحبُّ الدّجاج بالرّزِّ أم بالزّيتون ؟

3 Do you like chicken with rice or with olives ?

٤- أفضّلُ السّمك مع طماطم

4 I prefer fish with tomatoes.

182

٥ـ لا نحبُّ الرزَّ بلا زبيب

5 We don't like rice without (raisins.)

٦ـ هل يمكن أن تغيّرَ لي الصّحن
و أدواتِ الأكل ؟

6 Can you (is it possible that you) change the plate and the tableware for me ?

٧ـ هل يمكن أن تعطيَني فوطةً أخرى ؟

7 Can you (is it possible that you) give me another napkin ?

٨ـ هناك كثيرٌ مِنَ الوجبات فوقَ المائدة

8 There (are) many dishes on the table.

GRAMMAR : Verbs

The **completed aspect** of **EAT** ('akala) (Root : '-K-L)

I ate	'akal**tu**	أكلتُ
You [masc.] ate	'akal**ta**	أكلتَ
You [fem.] ate	'akal**ti**	أكلتِ
He ate	'akala	أكلَ
She ate	'akal**at**	أكلت
We ate	'akal**na**	أكلنا
You ate	'akal**tum**	أكلتم
They ate	'akal**u**	أكلوا

The **completed aspect** (singular only) of OPEN (fataḥa)
(Root : F-T-Ḥ)

I opened	fataḥtu	فتحت
You [masc.] opened	fataḥta	فتحت
You [fem.] opened	fataḥti	فتحت
He opened	fataḥa	فتح
She opened	fataḥat	فتحت

الدَّرسُ الحادي و الثَّلاثون

'ad-darsu l'ḥaadi wath-thalaathoon

في المطعم

١ـ بعد ذلك ، سآخذ تحلية ؛
ماذا عندكم؟(1)

٢ـ عندنا حلويات شرقيّة
متنوّعة

٣ـ كعب غزال و حلويات
بِاللّوز(2) و العسل

184

The lesson the first and the thirtieth

Pronounce : fi l-mat$^\epsilon$am
English : In the restaurant

1 Jaak   *Pronounce* : ba$^\epsilon$da dhaalik, sa'aakhudh tahliya ; maadha $^\epsilon$indakum (1) ?

Jack   *English* : After that, I'll take a dessert. What have you (1) ?

2 'al gharsoon   *Pronounce* : $^\epsilon$indana halawiyyaat sharqiyya mutanawwi$^\epsilon$a

The waiter   *English* : We have Middle Eastern pastries of different sorts.

3 'al gharsoon   *Pronounce* : ka$^\epsilon$b ghazaal wahalawiyyaat billawz (2) wal-$^\epsilon$asal

The waiter   *English* : Gazelle horns [a crescent-shaped cookie] and almond (2) and honey cakes.

185

٤ـ وكذلك عندنا فواكه و
سلطة برتقال

٥ـ حسنًا ! هاتِ © كعب غزال
و سلطة برتقال

٦ـ هل تشرب قهوة أم
شايًا بالنَّعناع ؟

٧ـ شايًا بالنَّعناع ، طبعًا !

(جاك ينتهي من الأكل و يطلب
قائمة الحساب)

٨ـ الحساب ، من فضلك !

٩ـ حالًا ، يا سيّدي

4 'al gharsoon
The waiter

Pronounce : wakadhaalik ^εindana fawaakih wasalata(t) burtuqaal !
English : We also have fruits and (an) orange salad.

5 Jaak
Jack

Pronounce : ḥasanan. haati (3) ka^εb ghazaal wasalata(t) burtuqaal
English : Good. Bring me (3) (a) gazelle horn and (an) orange salad.

6 'al gharsoon
The waiter

Pronounce : hal tashrab qahwa 'am shaay(an) bin-na^εnaa^ε ?
English : Do you drink coffee or mint tea ?

7 Jaak
Jack

Pronounce : shaay(an) bin-na^εnaa^ε tab^εan.
English : Mint tea, of course.

(Jaak yantahi mina l-'akl wayatlub qaa'imata l-ḥisaab)
(Jack finishes his meal (his eating) and asks for the bill)

8 Jaak
Jack

Pronounce : 'al ḥisaab, min faḍlik !
English : The bill, please.

9 'al gharsoon
The waiter

Pronounce : haalan, ya sayyidi
English : Right away, sir.

187

(يقدّم لهُ الحساب)

١٠ ـ تفضّل !

(جاك ينظر في قائمةِ الحساب)

١١ ـ هذا رخيص ؛ ألخدمة محسوبة ؟

١٢ ـ معلوم ! كلُّ شيٍء محسوب

(جاك يدفع)

١٣ ـ تفضّل ! و هذه زيادة لك !

١٤ ـ لا، شكراً ... إلى اللّقاء يا سيّدي !

(yuqaddim lahu l-ḥisaab)
(He presents the bill to him.)

10   'al gharsoon   *Pronounce* : tafaddal
       The waiter   *English* : Here you are.

(Jaak yanẓur fi qaa'imati l-ḥisaab)
(Jack examines the bill.)

11   Jaak   *Pronounce* : haadha rakhees ; 'al
                     khidma maḥsooba ?
       Jack   *English* : It's inexpensive ; (is) the
                     service included ?

12   'al gharsoon   *Pronounce* : ma^ϵloom. kullu shay'
                     maḥsoob
       The waiter   *English* : Of course. Everything is
                     included.

(Jaak yadfa^ϵ)
(Jack pays.)

13   Jaak   *Pronounce* : tafaddal. wahaadhihi
                     ziyaada lak
       Jack   *English* : Here you are. And here is
                     something extra for you.

14   'al gharsoon   *Pronounce* : la, shukran.. 'ila l-liqaa'
                     ya sayyidi.
       The waiter   *English* : No, thank you...Good-bye,
                     sir.

NOTES

1 The plural form, maadha ᶜindakum ‏ماذا عندكم؟‏ is used here for the same reason as in Lesson 2, Sentence 6 : Jack is not asking the waiter what *he* has, but what *they* (the restaurant people) have.

2 "Almond cakes" is written, as you see, "cakes with almond", **bil-lawz** ‏بالّلوز‏ , the word for "almond" being in the singular even though many almonds are involved. We similarly say of a pie made with many apples that it is an "apple pie". The "collective" or generic names for practically all fruits and vegetables in Arabic are masculine singulars. (The same is true of fish, animals — e.g. sheep — and of natural objects — e.g. trees, rocks, etc.) Here are some examples :

lemons	laymoon	‏ليمون‏
oranges	burtuqaal	‏برتقال‏
dates	tamr	‏تمر‏
beans	fool	‏فول‏

If we want to speak of *one* lemon, *one* orange, etc., we have to add to the word the feminine singular ending, **taa' marboota** ‏ة ــة‏

| a lemon | laymoona(tun) | ‏ليمونة‏ |
| an orange | burtuqaala(tun) | ‏برتقالة‏ |

We do the same if we want to designate *a* fish, *a* sheep, *a* tree, *a* rock.

3 The expression (an interjection) used here for "bring", **haati** ‏هات‏ ,is invariable, like such English expressions as "Look sharp !" or "Move along !" You will hear it often, especially in restaurants and cafés.

EXERCISES

‏١- أمس، أكلنا حلويات لذيذة‏

1 Yesterday, we ate (some) delicious pastries.

190

٢- يُفَضِّلُ الشَّايَ على القهوة

2 He prefers tea to coffee.

٣- هل الخدمة محسوبة دائماً ؟

3 Is the service always included ?

٤ ـ قبل التّحلية ، هات الجبنَ !

4 Before the dessert, bring the cheese.

٥ ـ أطلبِ القائمةَ من الغرسون

5 Ask the waiter for the menu,
(Request the menu from the waiter.)

٦- هل عندك صرف ؟

6 Have you (any) change ?

٧ ـ أينَ المرحاض ؟

7 Where is the toilet ?

٨ ـ حتّى أيِّ وقتٍ تقدّمونَ الطّعام

في المساء ؟

8 Until what time do you [plur.] serve (food) in the evening ?

191

GRAMMAR : Verbs

The **pending aspect** (indicative, singular) of three more verbs.

LOOK (naẓara) (Root : N-Ẓ-R)

I look	'anẓuru	أنظر إلى
You [masc.] look	tanẓuru	تنظر ″
You [fem.] look	tanẓureena	تنظرين ″
He looks	yanẓuru	ينظر ″
She looks	tanẓuru	تنظر ″

ASK (ṭalaba) (Root : Ṭ-L-B)

I ask	'aṭlubu	أطلب
You [masc.] ask	taṭlubu	تطلب
You [fem.] ask	taṭlubeena	تطلبين
He asks	yaṭlubu	يطلب
She asks	taṭlubu	تطلب

الدَّرسُ الثَّاني و الثَّلاثون

'ad-darsu th-thaani wath-thalaathoon

في الفندق

(في اليومِ التّالي صباحًا ...
ألخادم يطرقُ البابَ)

192

DRINK (shariba) (Root : SH-R-B)

I drink	'ashrabu
You [masc.] drink	tashrabu
You [fem.] drink	tashrabeena
He drinks	yashrabu
She drinks	tashrabu

COMMENTS

As in English, the verb "look" in Arabic is given different shades of meaning by the prepositions that are used with it :

I look at :   'anzur 'ila

I look into :   'anzur fi

The latter construction is also used (as in this lesson) to mean "examine" or "study" or "scrutinize".

Lesson 32

The lesson the second and the thirtieth

Pronounce : fi l-funduq
English : In the hotel

(fil-yawmi t-taali sabaahan... 'al khaadim yatruqu l-baab)
(The next morning (in the following day in the morning)...
The valet knocks at the door.)

193

١- تفضّل !

(يدخلُ الخادم)

٢- صباحَ الخير ، يا سيّدي !

٣- صباحَ النّور !

٤- كيف قضيت هذه اللّيلة[0] !

٥- بخير ، أحمدُ لِلّه[C] ...

كمِ السّاعة ؟

٦- السّاعة الثّامنة و النّصف ...

أقدّمُ لكَ الفطور

1 Jaak   *Pronounce* : tafaḍḍal !
   Jack   *English* : Come in !

(yadkhulu l-khaadim)
(The valet comes in (Comes in the valet).)

2 'al khaadim   *Pronounce* : ṣabaaḥa l-khayr, ya sayyidi
   The valet   *English* : Good morning, sir.

3 Jaak   *Pronounce* : ṣabaaḥa n-noor
   Jack   *English* : Good morning.

4 'al khaadim   *Pronounce* : kayfa qaḍayta haadhihi
                    l-layla (1) ?
   The valet   *English* : Did you sleep well (how did
                    you pass this night) (1) ?

5 Jaak   *Pronounce* : bikhayr, 'al-ḥamdu lillaah
                    (2) kami s-saaᶜa ?
   Jack   *English* : Very well, by the grace of God
                    (2). What time is it ?

6 'al khaadim   *Pronounce* : 'as-saaᶜa 'ath-thaamina wan-
                    nisf.. 'uqadimm(u) laka l-fuṭoor.
   The valet   *English:* It (is) half past eight (the hour (is)
                    the eighth and the half) ; here is your
                    breakfast (I serve you the breakfast.)

٧ ـ ماذا أحضرت لِلأكل ؟

٨ ـ قهوة بحليب مع خبز و
زبدة و عسل ، كما طلبت
أمس

٩ ـ و هذه صحيفةُ اليوم

١٠ ـ شكرًا ! ما هي الأخبار ؟

١١ ـ لا أدري ، يا سيّدي

١٢ ـ كيف حالُ الطَّقسِ اليوم ؟

7   Jaak   *Pronounce* : maadha 'aḥdarta lil-'akl ?

       Jack   *English* : What have you brought to eat (for the eating) ?

8   'al khaadim   *Pronounce* : qahwa biḥaleeb ma$^{\epsilon}$a khubz wazubda wa$^{\epsilon}$asal, kama (3) talabta 'ams

       The valet   *English* : Coffee with milk, with bread, butter and honey, as (3) you requested yesterday.

9   'al khaadim   *Pronounce* : wahaadhihi ṣaheefatu (4) l-yawm

       The valet   *English* : And this is today's newspaper (4).

10   Jaak   *Pronounce* : shukran ! ma hiya l-'akhbaar ?

       Jack   *English* : Thank you. What (is in) the news ?

11   'al khaadim   *Pronounce* : la 'adri (5), ya sayyidi

       The valet   *English* : I don't know (5), sir.

12   Jaak   *Pronounce* : kayfa ḥaalu t-taqsi l-yawm ?

       Jack   *English* : How is the weather (the state of the weather) to-day ?

١٣ ـ جميل جداً أتمنى لك
نهاراً⑥ سعيداً إن شاء الله⑦!

١٤ ـ إن شاء الله!

NOTES

1 This looks easy. It isn't. A few comments are needed :

(a) The expression "this night" — **haadhihi l-layla(t)** — usually means, in Arabic as in most European languages, the night that has ended or that is now in progress, not the one that will follow this evening.

(b) We saw in Lesson 31, Note 2, the difference between the *generic* words for lemons, oranges, fish, sheep, trees, and so on, and the words for *specific* lemons, oranges, fish, etc. The first are collective words, treated grammatically as masculine singulars. If we want them to designate individual things, we have to add to them the feminine singular ending in **taa' marboota**. There are some other words in Arabic that behave in a similar way. One of them is the word for "night". The generic word for "night" in the sense of "night-time" (hours of darkness) is the masculine singular collective,

layl(un) ليل . It is made to mean a particular night by the addition of the **taa' marboota** ending. "*The* night" is thus **'al-layla(t)**; and "*this* night", as in the present instance, is accordingly **haadhihi l-layla(t)** هذه الليلة .

(c) To say "*at* night" or "*by* night", we add to the generic word **layl** the adverbial case-ending -an, and we obtain **laylan** ليلاً .

2 It is the usual practice to complete the expression for "well" or "very well", **bi-khayr** بخير , with "by the grace of Allah", **'al hamdu li-llaah.** This is merely giving credit where it is due.

3 This is a convenient occasion to look at the ways of saying in Arabic "like", "as" and "as if".

(a) To say that someone or something is *like* someone or something else (necessarily a **noun** or a word assimilated to a noun), we use the preposition **ka** ك . For example :

198

13 'al khaadim   *Pronounce* : jameel jiddan.. 'atamanna lak(a) nahaar(an) (6) sa^ϵeed(an) 'in shaa'a l-llaah (7)

     The valet   *English* : Lovely (very beautiful)... I wish you a pleasant (happy) day (6), God willing (7).

14 Jaak   *Pronounce* : 'in shaa'a l-llaah
     Jack   *English* : God willing.

✳

Like this hotel   **kahaadha l-funduq**   كهذا الفندق

(Notice the importance of the word order here : If we said, **funduq(un) kahaadha,** it would mean, "a hotel like this" or "such a hotel".

You will encounter some idiomatic expressions in which Arabic uses a construction with "like" where we would use one with "as" :

As usual   **kal^ϵaada**   كالعادة
(Like the habit)

(b) To say that someone or something is like *him* or *it* (or another **pronoun**), we cannot use **ka,** which takes nouns only.
Instead, we must use **mithla**   مثل   , which can take *either* nouns or attached pronouns :

Like me   **mithli**   مثلي

Like you   **mithlak**   مثلك

Like this city   **mithla haadhihi l-madeena**

                               مثل هذه المدينة.

(Like many other prepositions, **mithla** is in fact a noun — **mithl(un),** meaning "likeness" or "similarity" — "frozen" with its object/ adverb case ending **-a.**)

(c) The word for "as" is **kama**   كما . It is always followed by a verb (which contains a subject pronoun) :

As you wish   **kama tureed**   كما تريد

(d) To say, "As the Board Chairman wishes" (in which "as" seems, in English, to be followed by a *noun* which is the subject of the verb), we merely respect the customary Arabic practice of putting

199

the verb *before* its subject, and we come back to (c) : "As wishes the Board Chairman".

(e) "As if", in Arabic, is a combinaition of **ka** with **'anna : ka'anna**

كَأَنَّ . Before we look at the curious behavior of this word, you should refer back to Lesson 19, Note 1, in which we discussed the similarly curious behavior of the Arabic word "but", **laakinna**. (The words **'inna** and **'anna** are closely related.) Just as **laakinna** exerts a "butting" action on the word that follows it, **ka'anna** exerts what we may call an "as-iffing" action. The word that follows it, being the object of this action, must therefore, again, be either a noun in the object case or an attached object-pronoun, *even though this noun or pronoun is in turn the subject of a verb :* "As if the **boss intended** to give me a raise", or "As if **I had** another job waiting". Both "the boss" and "I" are here "as-iffed".

4 **ṣaheefa** (a synonym of **jareeda**), means a newspaper, a sheet (of paper) or a page (of a book). From the same root are derived the words for "journalism" or "press" — صِحَافَةٌ — **sahaafa(tun)** and for "journalist" — **sahafi(yyun)** صَحَفِي .

5 The expression **la 'adri** is an up-in-the-air way of saying "I don't know". That is, it doesn't apply to anything in particular. You cannot use it to say, "I don't know Muhammad" or "I don't know this part of town". For that purpose, you have to use **la 'a$^\epsilon$rif** لا أَعْرِف .

6 We looked at "night" in Note 1 ; now we will look at "day".

(a) The generic term for "day" in the sense of "daytime" (that is, the daylight hours) is **nahaar**. Its opposite is **layl(un)**.

(b) The specific word for *"a* day", from morning to evening, is **yawm** يَوْم . Its opposite is **layla(t)**.

(c) However, just as in English, the same word, **yawm**, is also used to mean a full twenty-four hour day (which in the Arab countries begins and ends at sunset, not at midnight).

(d) An adverbial ending can be put on the Arabic generic words for both night and day :

Night and day   **laylan wanahaar(an)**   لَيْلاً و نَهَارًا

7 Almost any remark related to the future is apt to be completed by the knock-on-wood expression, **'inshaa'allaah**, "If Allah so wills". As a reply to "We'll meet at eight in the Flamingo Bar", it is a very convenient way of saying. "Provided that you don't

200

change your mind, that I don't have to work late, and that neither of us is run over by a drunken cab driver between now and then."

EXERCISES

١- كيف قضيت عطلتك ؟

1 How did you spend your vacation ?

٢- هل تدري أين شارعُ الزّهور ؟

2 Do you know where Flower Street (is) ?

٣- ما طلبت منكم شئاً

3 I didn't ask you for anything.
(Not I asked of you something.)

٤- هذا المطعم مغلق ليلاً ،
كما تعرفون

4 This restaurant is closed at night, as you [plur.] know.

GRAMMAR : Verbs

The **completed aspect** (singular) of three more verbs.

BRING ('ahdara) (Root : H-D-R)

I brought	'ahdartu	أحضرت
You [masc.] brought	'ahdarta	أحضرت
You [fem.] brought	'ahdarti	أحضرت
He brought	'ahdara	أحضر
She brought	'ahdarat	أحضرت

ASK (talaba) (Root : T-L-B)

I asked	talabtu	طلبت
You [masc.] asked	talabta	طلبت
You [fem.] asked	talabti	طلبت

201

| He asked | talaba | طَلَب |
| She asked | talabat | طَلَبَت |

SPEND or **PASS** (qada) (in the sense of "spend time")
(Root : Q-D-Y)

I spent	qadaytu	قَضَيتُ
You [masc.] spent	qadayta	قَضَيتَ
You [fem.] spent	qadayti	قَضَيتِ
He spent	qada	قَضَى
She spent	qadat	قَضَت

الدَّرسُ الثَّالِثُ والثَّلاثُونَ

'ad-darsu th-thaalith wath-thalaathoon

مُخابَرَةٌ هاتِفِيَّةٌ

(يَدِقُّ جِرسُ الهاتِفِ... جاكَ
يَرفَعُ السَّمّاعَةَ)

١ـ أَلو... مَنْ① يَتَكَلَّم ؟

٢ـ أَلو ! لا أَسمَع جَيِّدًا ...
مَن يَتَكَلَّم ؟

202

The lesson the third and the thirtieth

Pronounce : mukhaabara haatifiyya
English : A telephone call

(yaduqqu jarasu l-haatif... Jaak yarfa$^\epsilon$u s-sammaa$^\epsilon$a)
(The (bell of the) telephone rings... Jack picks up the receiver.)

1 Jaak   *Pronounce* : 'aaloo.. man (1) yatakallam ?
   Jack   *English* : Hello ! Who (1) is speaking ?

2 Jaak   *Pronounce* : 'aaloo ! la 'asma$^\epsilon$(u) jayyidan.. man yatakallam ?
   Jack   *English* : Hello ! I can't hear you well... Who is speaking ?

203

٣ـ آه! السّيّد نبيـل! أهلاً! كيف الصّحّة؟

٤ـ بخير ... هل قضيت ليلةً مريحةً؟

٥ـ نعم، كنت تعبان بعد هذا السّفر

٦ـ هل لقيت مطعمًا جيّدًا، مساءَ أمس؟

٧ـ نعم، أكلت في مطعم الواحة، قريبًا منَ الفندق

٨ـ هل تعرفهُ؟

٩ـ طبعًا ... هو مشهور جدًّا ... كيف كان الطّعام؟

١٠ـ لذيذًا و رخيصًا

3 Jaak *Pronounce* : 'aah ! as-sayyid nabeel ! 'ahlan ! kayfa s-sihha ?

  Jack *English* : Ah ! Mr Nabeel ! Good morning (welcome) ! How are you (how the health) ?

4 'ahmad *Pronounce* : bikhayr... hal qadayta layla(tan) mureeha (2) ?

  Ahmad *English* : Well... Did you have (spend) a restful (2) night ?

5 Jaak *Pronounce* : na€am, kuntu ta€baan ba€da haadha s-safar

  Jack *English* : Yes, I was tired, after the (this) trip.

6 'ahmad *Pronounce* : hal laqeeta mat€am(an) jayyid(an) masaa'a 'ams ?

  Ahmad *English* : Did you find a good restaurant last night ?

7 Jaak *Pronounce* : na€am, 'akaltu fi mat€ami l-waaha, qareeban mina l-funduq

  Jack *English* : Yes, I ate at the Oasis Restaurant, near the hotel.

8 Jaak *Pronounce* : hal ta€rifuhu ?

  Jack *English* : Do you know it [masc.] ?

9 'ahmad *Pronounce* : tab€an.. huwa mashhoor jiddan.. kayfa kaana t-ta€aam ?

  Ahmad *English* : Of course ! It is very well known. How was the food ?

10 Jaak *Pronounce* : ladheedh(an) warakhees(an) (3)

  Jack *English* : Delicious and inexpensive (3).

205

NOTES

1 The interrogative pronoun "Who ?" is **man** من , ("What ?" is **ma** ? or **maadha** ?) It is used in much the same way as in English, for both direct and indirect questions :

Who came ? **man waṣala ?** من وصل ؟

Do you know **hal tadri man yatakallam ?**
who is speaking ? هل تدري من يتكلم ؟

The same word, **man,** is also used as a *subject*-pronoun in statements, meaning "whoever" or "whosoever" :

Whoever works, **man yaᶜmal yanjaḥ** من يعمل ينجح
succeeds

Only rarely, in modern Arabic, is **man** من used as a *relative* pronoun. The relative "who" or "that", which we will look at more closely later, is **'alladhi** [masc.] or **'allati** [fem.]. Here are a couple of examples. You will notice, in both of them, the disappearance of the initial **'a**, as explained in Lesson 15, Note 3.

It (is) he who came **huwa lladhi jaa'a** هو الذي جاء

The town that I **'al madeena(tu) llati zurtuha**
visited. المدينة التي زرتها

2 Arabic nights, like nights elsewhere, can be "good" in various ways. But asking someone whether he has spent a night that was good because comfortable is not quite the same thing as wishing him "Good night !" with the expressions that we saw in Lessons 20 and 24 :

Good night **layla saᶜeeda** ليلة سعيدة
(Happy night)
Good night **layla mubaaraka** ليلة مباركة
(Blessed night)

3 The object-case endings on the adjectives here are required by the implied verb, "was" **kaana**, which, as you will recall, takes a direct object in the same way as "throw" or "hit". The food *was* delicious and inexpensive.

206

EXERCISES

1 Who is asking (for) me ?

١- مَنْ يَطْلُبُني ؟

2 Whom (do) you want to (that you) talk to ?

٢- مَعَ مَنْ تُريدُ أَنْ تَتَكَلَّمَ ؟

3 The line is busy ; she has been talking (since) a long time.

٣- الخَطُّ مَشْغُول ؛ هِيَ تَتَكَلَّم مُنْذُ زَمَنٍ طَويل

4 May I (is it possible that I) talk to (with) Mr Jawaad ?

٤- هَلْ يُمْكِنُ أَنْ أَتَكَلَّمَ مَعَ السَّيِّد جواد ؟

5 He is not in (not present).

٥- لَيْسَ مَوْجودًا

6 No matter... I will call him tomorrow.

٦- لا يُهِمّ... سَوْفَ أُخَابِرُهُ غَدًا

٧ ـ هذا الرّقم غير صحيح

7 It is a wrong number.
(This number not correct.)

٨ ـ ما عندي هاتف في البيت

8 I have no telephone at home (in the house).

٩ ـ ولكن ، يمكنُكَ أن تخابرَني في المكتب

9 But you can (it is possible that you) phone me at the office.

الدّرسُ الرّابعُ والثّلاثون

'ad-darsu r-raabi$^\epsilon$ wath-thalaathoon

مخابرة هاتفيّة

١ ـ وأنت ؟ كيف حالُ عائلتك ؟

٢ ـ كلّهُم ① بخير ، ألحمدُ للّه .
ننتظر زيارتَكَ اليوم

٣ ـ متى ؟

208

١٠ ـ لا تقطع !

10   Don't hang up (cut).

١١ ـ قطعوا الخطّ

11   We have been cut off (they have cut the line).

Lesson 34

The lesson the fourth and the thirtieth

Pronounce : mukhaabara haatifiyya
English : A telephone call

1 Jaak 'ila 'ahmad Jack to Ahmad	*Pronounce* : wa 'anta ? kayfa haal(u) ^ᵉaa'ilatik ? *English* : And you ? How (is) your family (How the state of your family) ?
2 'ahmad Ahmad	*Pronounce* : kulluhum (1) bikhayr, 'al-hamd(u) li-llaah [*or* : 'al hamdu l-llaah] nantazir ziyaaratak(a) l-yawm *English* : They (are) all (1) well, God be praised. We are expecting your visit today.
3 Jaak Jack	*Pronounce* : mata ? *English* : When ?

209

٤ـ عندما تحبّ

٥ـ سوف أتغدّى حول الواحدة
بعد الظُّهر و سأكونُ
عندكم^⑤ في الثّالثة
٦ـ حسنًا ! ننتظرُك إذن

٧ـ مع الأسف ، لا يمكن أن
أخذَك بسيّارتي ؛
خذ تاكسي

٨ـ عندك عنواني : شارعُ الزّهور
رقم : ستّةَ عَشَرَ

٩ـ خلفَ^③ قصرِ الثّقافة ...
إلى اللّقاء يا أخي^④

4 'aḥmad   *Pronounce* : ^ϵindama tuḥibb
Ahmad   *English* : When you like.

5 Jaak   *Pronounce* : sawfa 'ataghadda ḥawla l-waahida ba^ϵda z-zuhr wasa'akoonu ^ϵindakum (2) fi th-thaalitha
Jack   *English* : I'll have lunch at about one (after noon) and I'll be at your place (2) at three.

6 'aḥmad   *Pronounce* : ḥasanan ! nantaziruk 'idhan
Ahmad   *English* : Good ! In that case we'll be expecting you.

7 'aḥmad   *Pronounce* : ma^ϵa l'asaf, la yumkin 'an 'aakhudhak bisayyaarati. khudh taaksi
Ahmad   *English* : Unfortunately, I can't (it is not possible that I) fetch you with my car. Take a taxi.

8 'aḥmad   *Pronounce* : ^ϵindak ^ϵunwaani : shaari^ϵu z-zuhoor, raqm sittata ^ϵashara
Ahmad   *English* : You have my address : Flower Street, number 16.

9 'aḥmad   *Pronounce* : khalfa (3) qaṣri th-thaqaafa... 'ila l-liqaa', ya 'akhi (4)
Ahmad   *English* : Behind (3) the Cultural Center (Palace of Culture)... Good-bye, my friend (brother) (4).

211

١٠ - إلى اللّقاء ، و شكرًا

★

rious forms, uses and shades of meaning :
ll of them'', in the plural.
'each'' or ''every'', when it is used with a sin-
efinite article :

kull(u) $^\epsilon$aa'ila(tin)   كلُّ عائلـة

Each (or every) restaurant   kull(u) mat$^\epsilon$am(in)   كلُّ مطعم

(c) If kull is used with a singular noun having the definite article,
it means ''whole'' or ''entire'' :

The whole family   kullu l-$^\epsilon$aa'ila(ti)   كلُّ العائلـة

The entire restaurant   kullu l-mat$^\epsilon$am(i)   كلُّ المطعم

(d) When the noun that kull is used with is a plural with the definite
article, is has the plural sense of ''all the'' :

All the people   kullu n-naas(i)   كلُّ النّاس

All the offices   kullu l-makaatib(i)   كلُّ المكاتب

All the cars   kullu s-sayyaaraat(i)   كلُّ السّيّارات

212

10 Jaak   *Pronounce* : ila l-liqaa' washukran !
     Jack   *English* : Good-bye and thank you.

★

(e) If we want to *emphasize* the idea of wholeness or entireness or unanimity, we can do so by putting **kull** *after* the noun and by attaching to it, for further emphasis, the pronoun corresponding to the noun :

The *entire* day	'al-yawm kulluhu	أليوم كلّه
The *whole* family	'al-ᶜaa'ila kulluha	ألعائلة كلها
All the people	'an-naas kulluhum	النّاس كلهم
All of us	naḥnu kulluna	نحن كلّنا
All of you	'antum kullukum	أنتم كلّكم

2 You will easily recognize here another common shade of meaning of the preposition ᶜ**inda** when completed by an attached pronoun. Here, ᶜ**inda**, plus **kum**, gives ᶜ**indakum** عندكم meaning "at your place". The "your" is plural because it is the whole family's place.

3 The preposition "behind" can be translated in Arabic either by **khalfa** خَلْفَ or by **waraa'a** وَرَاءَ .

4 The term **'akhi,** which means literally "my brother", is used to express close friendship.

EXERCICES

١- متى تريد أن نتغدّى ؟

1 When do you want to (have) lunch ?

٢- يمكن أن تنتظرُني في البيت

2 You can (it is possible that you) wait for me at home.

٣- سأكونُ عندك حوالي الساعة
الحادية عشرة صباحًا

3 I'll be at your place at about 11 in the morning.

٤- هل يمكن أن ينتظرَنا لزيارةِ
المدينة ؟

4 Can he wait for us to visit (for the visit of) the town ?

الدّرسُ الخامس و الثّلاثون

'ad-darsu l-khaamis wath-thalaathoon

مراجعة

214

٥ ـ نَتَغَدَّى عادةً في مطعمِ «الشَّلَّالِ» ،
خَلْفَ المَحْكَمةِ

5 We usually (have) lunch at the Cascade Restaurant, behind the Court House.

GRAMMAR : Verbs
Pending aspect of WAIT FOR, EXPECT ('intazara) (Root : N-Z̧-R)

I wait for	'antaziru	أُنْتَظِرُ
You [masc.] wait for	tantaziru	تَنْتَظِرُ
You [fem.] wait for	tantazireena	تَنْتَظِرِينَ
He waits for	yantaziru	يَنْتَظِرُ
She waits for	tantaziru	تَنْتَظِرُ

Lesson 35

The lesson the fifth and the thirtieth

Pronounce : muraaja$^\epsilon$a
English : Review

In this lesson we will take a closer and more systematic look at a few matters that we have dealt with until now in bits and pieces. To do so properly, we will have to introduce a few bits and pieces that you have not seen before but that present no special difficulty.

1 How to make a sentence negative

What is made negative in a sentence is the verb (which, in the case of noun-sentences, is merely *implied*). The ways in which verbs are made negative depend on whether they are in the **pending aspect** (and, if so, whether they are indicative, imperative or subjunctive, and whether they refer to present or future time) or in the **completed aspect** (real or imagined past time). We will deal with them accordingly.

Pending Aspect

(a) A simple statement (indicative) with an expressed verb is made negative just by placing before the verb the Arabic word for "no" or "not", **la** ﻻ .

I smoke **'udakhkhin(u)**   I don't smoke   **la 'udakhkhin(u)**

(b)   But if the statement is a noun-sentence there is no verb to which **la** can be applied. The noun-sentence corresponding to the example in (a) above, but with a specific sense of *present* action (rather than just of customary or habitual action), would be, "I (am) smoking". To make this negative, we use the convenient Arabic verb for "not to be", **laysa** (= "he is not"). Like **kaana** (the verb "to be" in its completed aspect), **laysa** is an "active" (transitive) verb ; the noun or adjective that completes it is therefore naturally in the object case [See Lesson 27, Note 4]. An odd feature of the verb **laysa** should be pointed out : **it exists only in its completed aspect,** as if the fact of "not being" something were necessarily an accomplished fact ; but it has the meaning of a verb in the pending aspect. It is conjugated on the model of **kaana**, as follows :

I am not	**lastu**
You [masc.] are not	**lasta**
You [fem.] are not	**lasti**
He is not	**laysa**
She is not	**laysat**
We are not	**lasna**
You are not	**lastum**
They are not	**laysu**

And here is an example of how to use it :

It [masc.] is not open   **laysa maftooḥan**

ليس مفتوحًا

(c) We saw in Lesson 27, Note 4, that another way to make a noun-sentence negative is to use the expression **ghayr** غَيـر "other than", followed (as if it were a preposition) by a noun or an adjective in the oblique case (of which the ending is rarely pronounced). Here is an example of this which we saw in Lesson 23, Note 4 :

It (is) possible   **haadha mumkin**

هذا ممكن

It (is) not possible   **haadha ghayr mumkin**
(= other than possible)

هذا غير ممكن

(d)   Another word for "not", used particularly with the expression for "have" that is made up of the preposition ᵉinda عند with an attached object-pronoun [See Lesson 7]," is **ma** ما . Here is an example of this that we saw on page 50 :

I have nothing to declare   **ma ᵉindi shay' mamnooᵉ**
(Not in my possession (is) something forbidden)

ما عندي شيء ممنوع

(e) We will see now, for the first time, how we negate a verb in the pending aspect when it refers to a *future* action. This is very simple. You know that, in the affirmative, the future sense is given to the verb by the prefix **sa**. To make the verb negative, we replace **sa** by a different particle,

lan لَنْ , which, when completed by a verb in the **subjunctive,** gives to it *both* a future *and* a negative sense :

| He will arrive | **sayaṣilu** | سيصل |
| He will not arrive | **lan yaṣila** | لن يصل |

(f) If we want to make negative a *command* (imperative) rather than a statement, we again ressort to **la,** but this time followed by a verb in the semi-imperative mood that we have baptized the "chopped-off" jussive :

| Don't leave ! | **la tadhhab** | لا تذهب ! |

(g) One other negative particle, **lam** لم acts in a peculiar way. When used with a verb in the *jussive mood* (hence necessarily in the pending aspect), it *both* makes the verb negative *and* gives to it a past (completed aspect) meaning :

| We didn't arrive | **lam naṣil** | لم نصل |

Completed Aspect

To make negative a verb in the completed aspect, we merely put the negative particle **ma** ما in front of it :

I didn't ask you **ma ṭalabtu minkum shay'an**
for anything

ما طلبت منكم شيئًا

We didn't arrive **ma waṣalna** ما وصلنا

2 The completed aspect of the verb

We have already encountered a number of verbs in the
completed aspect. It would be useful, at this stage, to define the regular "patterns" of the changes that they undergo
from person to person, just as we did in Lesson 7 for
verbs in the pending aspect.

In the singular

(a) The **first person** (I), whether **masculine** or **feminine**,
always ends in **-tu** تُ .

I arrived	waṣaltu	وصلتُ
I learned	ta$^\epsilon$allamtu	تعلّمتُ
I forgot	naseetu	نسيتُ
I ate	'akaltu	أكلتُ
I opened	fataḥtu	فتحتُ
I spent (time)	qaḍaytu	قضيتُ
I asked for	ṭalabtu	طلبتُ

(b) The **second person (you)**, when **masculine**, always ends in **-ta** ـْتَ .

You arrived	waṣalta	وَصَلْتَ
You learned	taᶜallamta	تَعَلَّمْتَ
You forgot	naseeta	نَسِيتَ
You ate	'akalta	أَكَلْتَ
You opened	fataḥta	فَتَحْتَ
You spent (time)	qaḍayta	قَضَيْتَ
You asked for	ṭalabta	طَلَبْتَ

(c) The **second person (you)**, when **feminine**, always ends in **-ti** ـْتِ .

You arrived	waṣalti	وَصَلْتِ
You learned	taᶜallamti	تَعَلَّمْتِ
You forgot	naseeti	نَسِيتِ
You ate	'akalti	أَكَلْتِ
You opened	fataḥti	فَتَحْتِ
You spent (time)	qaḍayti	قَضَيْتِ
You asked for	ṭalabti	طَلَبْتِ

220

(d) The **third person masculine (he)** always ends in **-a** ـَ .

He arrived	waṣala	وَصَلَ
He learned	ta^ϵallama	تَعَلَّمَ
He forgot	nasiya	نَسِيَ
He ate	'akala	أَكَلَ
He opened	fataḥa	فَتَحَ
He spent (time)	qaḍa	قَضَى
He asked for	ṭalaba	طَلَبَ

(e) The **third person feminine (she)** always ends in **-at** ـَتْ .

She arrived	waṣal**at**	وَصَلَتْ
She learned	ta^ϵallam**at**	تَعَلَّمَتْ
She forgot	nasiy**at**	نَسِيَتْ
She ate	'akal**at**	أَكَلَتْ
She opened	fataḥ**at**	فَتَحَتْ
She spent (time)	qaḍ**at**	قَضَتْ
She asked for	ṭalab**at**	طَلَبَتْ

In the plural (masculine forms only)

(f) The **first person (we)** always ends in -na نَا .

We arrived	waṣalna	وصلنا
We learned	taᵉallamna	تعلّمنا
We forgot	naseena	نسينا
We ate	'akalna	أكلنا
We opened	fataḥna	فتحنا
We spent (time)	qaḍayna	قضينا
We asked for	ṭalabna	طلبنا

(g) The **second person (you)** always ends in -tum تُمْ .

You arrived	waṣaltum	وصلتُمْ
You learned	taᵉallamtum	تعلّمتُمْ
You forgot	naseetum	نسيتُمْ
You ate	'akaltum	أكلتُمْ
You opened	fataḥtum	فتحتُمْ
You spent (time)	qaḍaytum	قضيتُمْ
You asked for	ṭalabtum	طلبتُمْ

222

(h)   The **third person (they)** always ends in -u وُ or in -aw اْوَ .

They arrived	waṣalu	وَصَلُوا
They learned	taᵉallamu	تَعَلَّمُوا
They forgot	nasaw	نَسَوْا
They ate	'akalu	أَكَلُوا
They opened	fataḥu	فَتَحُوا
They spent (time)	qaḍaw	قَضَوْا
They asked for	ṭalabu	طَلَبُوا

In the above table, we have omitted feminine forms (as well as duals) not for anti-feminist reasons but because they are not often encountered.

3 The particles " 'an" أَنْ and " 'anna" أَنَّ

These two similar words have somewhat different meanings and grammatical functions :

(a) As you already know, **'an** is the conjunction "that", used to introduce subordinate clauses governed by such main verbs as "it is necessary that", "I want that", "it is possible that", and so on. The verbs in these subordinate clauses, as you also know, are always in the subjunctive of the pending aspect. A typical example, just as a reminder, is :

He may be working (It is   **yumkin(u) 'an yaᵉmala**
possible that he is working)

223

(b)   The so-called "particle" (there is no other word

for it) 'anna أَنَّ is rather tricky. It is used in situations
where, in English, we might say, for example' "I know
of his doing something" or "I believe him *to be* someone";
and the grammatical construction that it requires is more
or less similar to the construction in English, as you will
see from the following examples :

I know of his arriving tomorrow.

'a^{ɛ}rif 'annahu yaṣil ghadan

(In this instance, 'anna is completed by the attached
object-pronoun **hu**, making "of his"; the verb is in the
indicative of the pending aspect, and its future sense is
made clear enough by **ghadan**, "tomorrow", so that we
don't need **sa**.)

I know the Oasis Restaurant   'a^{ɛ}rif 'anna mat^{ɛ}ama

to be far.   l-waaḥa ba^{ɛ}eed(un)

(In this instance, 'anna is completed by the *noun*, "restaurant", in the *object case*.)

الدَّرْسُ السَّادِسُ و الثَّلَاثُونَ

ad-darsu s-saadis wath-thalaathoon

فِي التَّاكْسِي

١ ـ تَاكْسِي !

٢ ـ نَعَم ، يَا سَيِّدِي . إِلَى أَيْنَ

أَنْتَ ذَاهِبٌ ①؟

224

The general "thought-process" (as we may call it) behind
the uses of 'an and 'anna is analagous to the one we discussed in Lesson 19 in relation to the words for "but", **laakin**

لكن and **laakinna** لكنّ .

لا يمكن أن آخذك
بسيّارتي ...

Lesson 36

The lesson the sixth and the thirtieth

Pronounce : fi t-taaksi
English : In the taxi

| 1 | Jaak | *Pronounce* : taaksi ! |
| | Jack | *English* : Taxi ! |

2 'as-saa'iq   *Pronounce* : na^εam, ya sayyidi ! 'ila
'ayna 'anta dhaahib ? (1)

The driver   *English* : Yes, sir ! Where (are) you
going ? (1)

225

٣ـ إلى شارعِ الزّهورِ، رقم:

سِتَّةَ عَشَرَ ... هل هو بعيد؟

٤ـ في وسطِ المدينة...

أنت فرنسيّ؟

٥ـ نعم، أنا من باريس

٦ـ أهلاً! بلادُكم© جميلة

٧ـ هل أنت هنا لِأُوّل مرّة©؟

٨ـ نعم، هذه هي المرّةُ الأولى

3 Jaak   *Pronounce* : 'ila shaari^εi z-zuhoor, raqm sittata ^εashara... hal huwa ba^εeed ?

Jack   *English* : To Flower Street, number sixteen... Is it far ?

4 'as-saa'iq   *Pronounce* : fi wasaṭi l-madeena... 'anta faransi ?

The driver   *English* : In the center of the town. You (are) French ?

5 Jaak   *Pronounce* : na^εam, 'ana min baarees

Jack   *English* : Yes, I (am) from Paris.

6 'as-saa'iq   *Pronounce* : 'ahlan ! bilaadukum (2) jameela

The driver   *English* : Welcome ! Your country (2) (is) beautiful .

7 'as-saa'iq   *Pronounce* : hal 'anta huna li'awwal marra (3) ?

The driver   *English* : Is this your first time here (you here for the first time) (3) ?

8 Jaak   *Pronounce* : na^εam, haadhihi hiya l-marra (tu) l-'oola

Jack   *English* : Yes, this (is) the first time.

227

٩ـ تتكلّمُ العربيّة جيّداً !

١٠ـ شكراً ! أحبُّ هذه اللّغة
كثيراً (٤)

١١ـ ولكن ، لا أتكلّم جيّداً ؛
أحتاجُ إلى ممارسة (٥)

١٢ـ هنا ستتكلّمُ العربيّة
دائماً

*

NOTES

1 Why do we here use the noun-sentence, "Where (are) you going ?" rather than the verb "to go" in its pending aspect, 'ila ayna

tadhhab ? إلى أين تذهب ؟ ? The difference between the two usages is this : The verb "to go" in its pending aspect and in this context can mean : "Where do you go ?" (every Sunday), or "Where are you going ?" (today or next week), or, if it is preceded by **sa**, "Where will you go ?" But the sense we want to convey here is : "Where are you **now in the act of going** ?" For this shade of meaning, it is preferable to use a noun-sentence made up just of a subject and an active participle, with no verb.

The active participle in a noun-sentence — in this case, "going" — has the same *immediacy* as would an adjective such as "hungry" or "exasperated" or "pleased" or "aghast".

9 'as-saa'iq *Pronounce* : tatakallamu l-ᵉarabiyya jayyidan

  The driver *English* : You speak Arabic well.

10 Jaak *Pronounce* : shukran. 'uḥibb(u) haadhihi l-lugha katheeran (4)

  Jack *English* : Thank you. I like this language very much (4).

11 Jaak *Pronounce* : walaakin, la 'atakallam jayyidan ; 'aḥtaaj 'ila mumaarasa (5)

  Jack *English* : But I don't speak (it) well ; I need practice (5).

12 'as-saa'iq *Pronounce* : huna satatakallamu l-ᵉarabiyya daa'iman

  The driver *English* : Here, you will speak Arabic all the time.

TO GO   راح يروح

As a second illustration, we will use an alternative word for "go" (or "leave"), the verb **raaḥa** (راح) , meaning "he went" or "he left". For the rather loose present or future sense, we again use (a) the present aspect of the verb ; for the immediate present sense, we use (b) a noun-sentence with an active participle :

(a) Where do you go ? **'ila 'ayna tarooḥ ?**   إلى أين تروح ؟

(b) Where are you now going ? **'ila 'ayna raa'iḥ ?**   إلى أين رائح ؟

2 Notice again here the plural "your", **-kum** كم rather than the singular **-k** ك . (The country in question is not just Jack's but that of all the people who live there.) Notice also the plural word for "country", **bilaad** [See Lesson 3, Note 2] and the use with it of a *feminine singular* adjective, **jameela**, required because it applies to the plural of an inanimate thing [See Lesson 9, Note 1].

229

3 The phrase, "the first time", **'awwal marra(tin)**, as written here, is a "yoked couple" [See page 70]. We will come back to this point in a moment ; and we will look first at a simpler way of saying the same thing :

(a) As you know, the adjective in Arabic normally comes after the noun that it qualifies ; it agrees with its noun in gender, number and case ; and it takes the definite article **'al** in the same way as its noun. We could therefore here compose "the first time" as follows :

The time [fem. noun]	**'al marra(tu)**	المرَّة
+ The first [fem. adj.]	**'al 'oola**	الأُولى
= The time the first	**'al marra l-'oola**	المرَّة الأُولى

We could apply the same principle to :

The last time	**'al marra l-'akheera**
(The time the last)	المرَّة الأخيـرة

(b) But we can also regard "the first time" as a yoked couple in the same way as "fruit juice" or "exit visa", in which an "of" is implied : "the first (of the) time". The implied "of" puts into the oblique case the feminine word for "time", **marra** مرَّة , which becomes **marra(tin)**. Because it is "yoked" to the preceding noun, "first", **'awwal** (which happens to be masculine), it makes this noun *definite* and thereby makes superfluous its definite article **'al**. The phrase, "the first time", hence becomes :

The first (of the) time	**'awwal marra(tin)**	أوَّل مرَّة

Applying the same principle to "the last time", we obtain :

The last (of the) time	**'aakhir marra(tin)**	آخِر مرَّة

(c) If we now apply each of the above two procedures to "the second time", we again obtain two different ways of saying the same thing :

The time the second	**'al marra th-thaaniya**	المرَّة الثانية

The second (of the) time   **thaani(ya) marra(tin)**

ثاني مرّة

4 The term "very much" has here, of course, an *adverbial* function (it qualifies the verb "to like"). But what serves as an adverb is in fact the adjective for "numerous" or "abundant" **katheer** كثير with the adverb-case ending **-an : katheeran** كثيراً . We might translate it as "abundantly". You will recall from Lesson 29, Note 1, that the word **jiddan** جدّاً also means "very" or "very much" ; and it is often used in place of **katheeran**.

5 The word for "practise", **mumaarasa** ممارسة is an example of what we have called a "verbal noun" or "gerund". It means literally "the practising" or "the exercising". We saw other examples of verbal nouns in Lesson 30, Note 3.

EXERCISES

١- هل أنت ذاهب إلى وسطِ
المدينة ؟

1 Are you [sing.] going to the center of (the) town ?

٢- هل تعرف هذا العنوان ؟

2 Do you [sing.] know this address ?

٣- أحبّ أن أتكلّم العربيّة ؛ وأنتَ،
هل تعلّمت الفرنسيّة ؟

3 I like to speak Arabic ; and you, have you learned French ?

٤- هناكَ كثيرٌ مِنَ السَّيّاراتِ

4 There are many cars there.

٥- أزورُ هذه المدينةِ للمرّةِ الثّالثةِ

5 I am visiting this town for the third time.

الدَّرسُ السَّابعُ و الثَّلاثون

'ad-darsu s-saabi⁶ wath-thalaathoon

في التّاكسي

١- اللّغةُ العربيّةُ جميلةٌ
ولكنّها صعبةٌ

٢- كَجميعِ اللّغاتِ ... أه،
ها هو شارعُ الزّهورِ

٣- سبعةٌ ... تسعةٌ ... أحدَ عشرَ.
ها قدْ وصلنا

٦- كم مرّة ذهب إلى المطعم الشَّرقيّ !

6 How many times has he gone to the Middle Eastern restaurant ?

٧- لم أتكلّم العربيّة منذ زمن طويل

7 I have not been speaking Arabic for long.

Lesson 37

The lesson the seventh and the thirtieth

Pronounce : fit-taaksi
English : In the taxi

1 Jaak

Jack

Pronounce : 'al lugha l-^ϵarabiyya jameela walaakinnaha sa^ϵba

English : The Arabic language is beautiful but it [fem.] (is) difficult.

2 'as-saa'iq

The driver

Pronounce : kajamee^ϵ(i) (1) l-lughaat(i)... 'aah ! ha huwa shaari^ϵu z-zuhoor

English : Like (I) all (the) languages... Ah ! here (is) Flower Street.

3 'as-saa'iq

The driver

Pronounce : sab^ϵa... tis^ϵa... 'ahada ^ϵashara ha qad (2) wasalna

English : Seven... nine... eleven... here we are (arrived).

233

٤ـ شكرًا ! كم، من فضلك ؟

٥ـ أربعة فرنكات [3] و ثلاثون
سنتيمًا [3]

٦ـ تفضّل ! هذه خمسة فرنكات

٧ـ مع الأسف ؟ ما عندي
صرف [4]

٨ـ لا يهمّ ... خذِ الباقي ...
مع السلامة !

٩ـ في الأمان !

234

4 Jaak

    Jack

Pronounce : shukran, kam, min faḍlik ?

English : Thank you. How much, please ?

5 'as-saa'iq

    The driver

Pronounce : 'arba^εatu farankaat (3) wathalaathoon santeem(an) (3)

English : Four Francs (3) and thirty centimes (3).

6 Jaak

    Jack

Pronounce : tafaḍḍal ! haadhihi khamsa(tu) farankaat

English : Here you are ; here are five Francs.

7 'as-saa'iq

    The driver

Pronounce : ma^εa l-'asaf ; ma ^εindi ṣarf (4)

English : I'm sorry (with the regret), I have no change (4).

8 Jaak

    Jack

Pronounce : la yuhimm... khudhi l-baaqi... ma^εa s-salaama !

English : No matter... Keep what's left (the rest). Good-bye.

9 'as-saa'iq

    The driver

Pronounce : fi l-'amaan

English : Good-bye.

NOTES

1 A couple of things should be noted here :

(a) The word used for "like", when we mean "like *something*" (i.e. a noun), is **ka** ﻙ . Being a preposition, it takes a noun in the oblique case. [See Lesson 32, Note 3].

(b) The word used here for "all" is **jamee**$^\epsilon$ جميع . This word is interchangeable with **kull** كل , which we studied in Lesson 34, Note 1. As used here, it is "yoked" to the word that follows and thereby made definite, so it doesn't itself need the definite article :

All (of) the languages   **jamee$^\epsilon$u l-lughaat(i)**   جميع اللّغات

2 With regard to **ha qad** : We saw in Lesson 6, Note 5, that the "particle" **qad** قد before a verb in the completed aspect emphasizes the completion of the act referred to, especially in the immediate past. The **ha** ها gives further emphasis to this, bringing the completion of the act up to the present and giving it the sense, in this instance, of "Here we are".

3 Here again, a harmless-looking sentence calls for several remarks :

(a) The word "Franc" is here in the plural because, as you will recall from Lessons 15 and 21, the numbers from 3 to 10 take a plural noun after them. As for "centimes", it is in the singular because (as you will also recall from Lesson 21) the numbers from 11 to 99 always take a singular noun with the indefinite adverb-case ending **-an** ; and here we have 30.

(b) The singular form of "Franc", a masculine noun, is **farank** فرنك . Here we see that its plural is **farankaat**. This type of "external" plural is normally used for feminine words whose singular ends in **taa' marbooṭa** ـة , that is, in **-at**. The plural endings are **-aatun** in the subject case and **-aatin** in the object/adverb and oblique cases. (The **t** of these endings is always pronounced, even though the case-ending which follows it may disappear in spoken Arabic.) Here are a couple of examples of such words :

	Singular	Plural	
Car	sayaara(tun) سيّارة	sayaaraat(un)	سيّارات
Lady	sayyida(tun) سيّدة	sayyidaat(un)	سيّدات

236

(c) But this "external feminine plural" is also commonly used for words of foreign origin (such as "Franc"). Other examples of this are :

Gram	ghraam	ghraam**aat**
Centimeter	santimitr	santimitr**aat**
Check	sheek	sheek**aat**
Dollar	doolaar	doolaar**aat**

(d) A number of other words of foreign origin, whose singulars can readily be assimilated to those of native Arabic words, behave like native words in that their plurals are formed by changes of *internal structure* rather than by the addition of external endings. A couple of examples are :

	Singular		**Plural**	
Doctor	**duktoor**	دكتور	dakaatira	دكاترة
Meter	**mitr**	متر	'amtaar	أمتار

(e) A final remark under this note : The Arab countries have so many different units of currency — dinars, dhirams, ryals, etc — that we will simplify matters in this book by sticking to Francs.

4 Notice the word that we have used for "change" : **ṣarf** صرف . This comes from the same root as the verb **ṣarrafa**, meaning "he changed" — but *only* in the sense of changing (or exchanging) *money*. The verb for "change" or "exchange" in a wider sense — clothes as well as money — is **ghayyara** (= "he changed"). We have already met both these roots in several forms in Lesson 12, where Jack exchanged his money. We there saw : **'aṣ-ṣarraaf**, "money-changer". But we also saw, as a term for "money exchange office" :

maktab **taghyeeri** n-nuqood   مكتب تغيير النّقود

This could just as well have been written : maktab **taṣreefi**

n-nuqood مكتب تصريف النّقود . But we cannot use the latter word in a non-monetary sense. We can *not* say with it, for example, "I change my clothes" : **'uṣarrif** malaabisi.

أصرف ملابسي   We have to say : **'ughayyir** malaabisi.

أغيّر ملابسي .

EXERCISES

١- هل عندك صرف ؟

1 Have you any small change ?

٢- هذه اللّغة ليست صعبة

2 This language is not difficult.

٣- سوف تتكلّمها بسرعة

3 You [masc.] will be speaking it in a short time (with speed).

٤- جميع الوجبات لذيذة

4 All the dishes are delicious.

٥- أعطني بقيّة الدّجاجة

5 Give me the rest of the chicken.

٦- منذ كم تدرس العربيّة ؟

6 How long have you been studying Arabic ?

٧- منذ ستّة أشهر

7 For (since) six months.

٨ ـ ستّة أَشهر فقط ؟

إِنّكَ تتكلّمُ جيّداً

8 Only six months ? You already speak (it) well.

٩ ـ يعودُ الفضلُ في ذلك

إلى الطّريقة "أسيميل"

9 Thanks to (the credit goes to) the "Assimil" method.

١٠ ـ إبني يتعلّمُ الفرنسيّة

بهذه الطّريقة هو الآخر

10 My son is also (he too) learning French by this method.

خذ الباقي

عند أحمد

(جاك ينظر إلى ساعتِهِ ①)

١- الثَّالثة إلّا الرّبعُ ... ماذا أعمل ؟... سأنتظر هنا

(يُفتَحُ الباب ويخرج أحمد)

٢- يا جاك ! ماذا تعمل أمامَ الباب ؟ تفضّل !

٣- جئتُ قبل الموعد ② ... ما أردت أن أزعجكم

The lesson the eighth and the thirtieth

Pronounce : ^ϵinda 'ahmad
English : In Ahmad's house (at Ahmad's)

(Jaak yanzur 'ila saa^ϵatihi) (1)
(Jack looks at his watch) (1)

1 Jaak   *Pronounce* : 'ath-thaalitha 'illa (2) r-rub^ϵ..
             maadha 'a^ϵmal ?... sa'antazir huna
  Jack   *English* : A quarter to (2) three. What
             shall I do ?... I'll wait here.

(yuftahu l-baab wayakhruj 'ahmad)
(The door opens (is opened) and Ahmad comes out.)

2 'ahmad *Pronounce* : ya Jaak ! maadha ta^ϵmal
             'amaama l-baab ?
  Ahmad   *English* : Jack ! What are you doing in
             front of the door ? Come in !

3 Jaak   *Pronounce* : ji'tu qabla l-maw^ϵid (3)...
             ma 'aradtu 'an 'uz^ϵijakum
  Jack   *English* : I got here (came) ahead of
             time (3). I didn't want to disturb you.

241

٤ ـ أبدًا ! تعالَ ! ننتظرك

بفارغِ الصّبرِ... تفضّل !

(يدخلانِ[٤] البيت)

٥ ـ أُقدّمُ[٥] لكَ اِبني الأكبرَ:[٦]

محمّد .

٦ ـ تشرّفنا !

٧ ـ تشرّفنا !

٨ ـ أينَ أمُّكِ و أختُكِ ؟

سنشربُ الشّاي مع السّيّد

« فرنوي »

٩ ـ هل تحبُّ الشّاي بالنّعناع

أم بدونِ[٧] نعناع ؟

4 'ahmad

Ahmad

Pronounce : 'abadan ! ta^εaala ! nanta-ziruk bifaarighi s-sabr... tafaddal !

English : Not at all ! Come... We have been waiting for you impatiently (with impatience)... Come in !

(yadkhulaani (4) l-bayt)
(They enter (4) the house)

5 'ahmad

Ahmad

Pronounce : 'uqaddim(u) (5) laka bni l-'akbar (6), muhammad

English : (May) I introduce (5) (to you) my eldest (6) son, Muhammad.

6 muhammad

Muhammad

Pronounce : tasharrafna

English : How do you do (it is an honor).

7 Jaak

Jack

Pronounce : tasharrafna

English : I am pleased to meet you.

8 'ahmad 'ila bnihi

Ahmad to his son

Pronounce : 'ayna 'ummuk wa'ukhtuk ? sanashrabu sh-shaay ma^εa s-sayyid ''firnuy''

English : Where (are) your mother and your sister ? we'll be having (drinking) tea with Monsieur Verneuil.

9 'ahmad 'ila Jaak

Ahmad to Jack

Pronounce : hal tuhibbu sh-shaay bin-na^εnaa^ε 'am bidooni (7) na^εnaa^ε ?

English : Do you like mint tea or (tea) without (7) mint ?

243

١٠ـ بالنّعناع ! لا أُشرب منه
كثيرًا في باريس

١١ـ ولكن ، شربتُ منه مساءً
الخميس في مطعم «الواحة»

1 The same word, saa$^\epsilon$a(tun) ساعة means both "watch" and the "hour" of the day that it tells.

2 We will divide this note into three parts :

(a) The word 'illa إلّا has the general meaning of "except (for)". When telling time, it thus means "minus" or "less" a certain part of the hour — hence, in English time-telling, "before" or "to" the hour in question. To say so many minutes *past* the hour, it is enough to use "and", wa. Here are some examples :

A quarter to ...	'illa r-rub$^\epsilon$	إلّا الرّبع
A quarter past ...	war-rub$^\epsilon$	والرّبع
Twenty to ... (*Less* the third)	'illa th-thulth	إلّا الثّلث
Twenty past (*And* the third)	wath-thulth	والثّلث
Half to ... (*Less* the half)	'illa n-nisf	إلّا النّصف
Half past (*And* the half)	wan-nisf	والنّصف

You will notice, in the above examples, that the word for "quarter" (one fourth) has the same root as the word for "four" r-b-$^\epsilon$, and

244

10 Jaak   *Pronounce* : bin-na[€]naa[€] ! la 'ashrab minhu katheeran fi baarees.

Jack   *English* : With mint. I don't drink much of it [fem.] in Paris

11 Jaak   *Pronounce* : walaakin, sharibtu minhu masaa'a l-khamees fi mat[€]ami l-waaha

Jack   *English* : But I drank some Thursday evening at the Oasis Restaurant.

that the word for "third" shares a root with the word for "three" : *th-l-th*. (But neither in Arabic nor in English is there any direct connection between the words for 2 and for 1/2.)

(b) This brings us to **fractions**. Here is a list of the commonest fractions, along with the corresponding cardinal numbers :

2	'ithnaan	إِثنَان	1/2	niṣf	نصف		
3	thalaatha	ثلاثة	1/3	thulth	ثلث		
4	'arba[€]a	أربعة	1/4	rub[€]	ربع		
5	khamsa	خمسة	1/5	khums	خمس		
6	sitta	ستة	1/6	suds	سدس		
7	sab[€]a	سبعة	1/7	sub[€]	سبع		
8	thamaaniya	ثمانية	1/8	thumn	ثمن		
9	tis[€]a	تسعة	1/9	tus[€]	تسع		
10	[€]ashra	عشرة	1/10	[€]ushr	عشر		

(c) **Telling time.** The barbarous if practical 24-hour time system, from midnight to midnight, is not generally used in the Arab world. One o'clock in the afternoon is not 1300 hours but I p.m. ("the

245

one after noon") :

الواحدة بعد الظهر

'al-waahida ba^{c}da z-zuhr

Six p.m. is not 1800 hours but "the sixth of the evening" :

السّادسة مساءً

'as-saadisa masaa'an

3 The "time" in question is of course "the time of the appointment", which is exactly what **maw^{c}id** موعد means.

4 The verb "enter" (or "go in" or "come in") takes a direct object just as it does in English. Because *two* people are entering, the *dual* form of the verb is used here :

يدخلانِ البيت

yadkhulaan(i) l-bayt.

5 We saw this verb in Lesson 23 with the sense of "serving" food. The basic sense of the root is "presenting" or "offering" ; here the presentation is an introduction. The verb is **qaddama** قدّم ("he presented").

6 This is the superlative of the adjective **'al kabeer : 'al 'akbar** الأكبر , meaning "the eldest" or "the biggest". (Like all adjectives, it comes after its noun, agrees with it in gender and has the definite article.) You will recall that, in Lesson 27, Note 4, we dealt with adjectives having the vowel pattern a-plus-a (states or conditions, infirmities, colors, comparatives and superlatives). Here are some examples of this pattern in superlatives :

The big	'al kabeer	الكبير
The biggest (eldest)	'al 'akbar	الأكبر
The small (young)	'as sagheer	الصّغير
The smallest (youngest)	'al 'asghar	الأصغر
The good (handsome)	'al hasan	الحسن
The best (handsomest)	'al 'ahsan	الأحسن

7 "Without" can be said either **bila** بلا , which you already know or **bidooni** بدون .

246

EXERCISES

١- مـن هو الأكبر ؟

1 Who is the eldest ?

٢- أُحِبُّ أَنْ أَقَدِّمَ لَكَ أَخِي عبدَ اللَّه

2 I'd like to (that I) introduce to you my brother Abdallah.

٣- تعالَ إلى البيتِ في الثانيةِ عشرةَ إلّا الثّلثِ

3 Come to the house at twenty to twelve (at the twelfth less the third).

٤- هي، جاءت بدونِ أمتعةٍ، وهو جاءَ بدونِ نقود

4 *She* came without luggage and *he* came without money.

٥- عندي موعد مع صديق ؛ ينتظرُني لتناولِ الغَداءِ

5 I have an appointment with a friend ; he is expecing me for lunch (for the taking of lunch).

٦- أَنتظِر زيارتَكَ بفارغِ الصَّبرِ

6 I am waiting for your visit with impatience.

247

٧ ـ عندنا موعد مع الطَّبيب

صباحَ الإِتنيــن

7 We have an appointment with the doctor Monday morning.

GRAMMAR : Verbs

The **completed aspect** (singular) of three more verbs.

COME (jaa'a) (Root : J-I-')

I came	ji'tu	جئتُ
You [masc.] came	ji'ta	جئتَ
You [fem.] came	ji'ti	جئتِ
He came	jaa'a	جاءَ
She came	jaa'at	جاءَت

DRINK (shariba) (Root : SH-R-B)

I drank	sharibtu	شربتُ
You [masc.] drank	sharibta	شربتَ
You [fem.] drank	sharibti	شربتِ
He drank	shariba	شربَ
She drank	sharibat	شربَت

248

WANT ('araada) (Root : R-W-D)

I wanted	'arad**tu**	أردتُ
You [masc.] wanted	'arad**ta**	أردتَ
You [fem.] wanted	'arad**ti**	أردتِ
He wanted	'araada	أراد
She wanted	'araada**t**	أرادت

عِند أحمد

(تدخل زوجة⁵ أحمد مع اِبنتِهِ⁶)

١ـ أُقدِّمُ لكَ زوجتي : ليلى
و اِبنتي : فاطمة

٢ـ تشرّفنا !

٣ـ مرحبًا ! كيف حالُك ؟

٤ـ بخير ، يا سيِّدتي

٥ـ أين مهدي و عبدُ اللّطيف ؟

250

The lesson the ninth and the thirtieth

Pronounce : [€]inda 'ahmad
English : In Ahmad's house (at Ahmad's)

(tadkhul (1) zawjatu 'ahmad ma[€]a bnatihi (2).)
(Ahmad's wife comes in (1) with his daughter (2).)

1 'ahmad 'ila
Jaak

Ahmad to
Jack

Pronounce : 'uqaddim(u) lak(a) zawjati, layla, wabnati, Faatima
English : (May) I introduce to you my wife, Layla, and my daughter, Fatima.

2 Jaak
Jack

Pronounce : tasharrafna
English : How do you do.

3 layla
Layla

Pronounce : marhaban ! kayfa haaluk ?
English : Welcome ! How are you ?

4 Jaak
Jack

Pronounce : bikhayr, ya sayyidati
English : (Very) well, Madame.

5 'ahmad

Ahmad

Pronounce : 'ayna mahdi wa[€]abdu l-lateef ?
English : Where (are) Mahdi and Abdul Latif ?

251

٦ - مهدي يلعب في البستان ؟
أمّا(٣) عبدُ اللّطيف فيلعب
بالكرة وراءَ البيت مع
أولادِ الجيران(٤)

٧ - لا يهمّ ... سأراهما(٥) في
مناسبةٍ أخرى، إن شاء اللّه !

٨ - يا فاطمة ! أحضري
الشّاي مع بعضِ(٦) الحلويات(٧)

٩ - وبعد ذلك ، سنقومُ(٨) معًا
بزيارةٍ حيٍّ من أحياءِ
المدينة.

6 layla

Pronounce : mahdi yal^εab fi l-bustaan ; 'amma (3) ^εabdu l-lateef fayal^εab bil-kura waraa'a l-bayt ma^εa 'awlaadi l- jeeraan (4)

Layla

English : Mahdi is playing in the garden ; as for (3) Abdul Latif, he is playing ball in back of the house with the neighbors' children (4).

7 Jaak

Pronounce : la yuhimm... sa'araahuma (5) fi munaasaba(tin) 'ukhra, 'in shaa'a l-llaah !

Jack

English : No matter... I'll see them both (5) on another occasion, I hope (if God so wishes).

8 'aḥmad 'ila faaṭima

Pronounce : ya faaṭima ! 'aḥdiri sh-shaay, ma^εa ba^εdi (6) l-ḥalawiyaat (7)

Ahmad to Fatima

English : Fatima ! Bring the tea with some (6) cakes (7).

9 'aḥmad multafitan 'ila Jaak

Pronounce : waba^εda dhaalik, sanaqoom(u) (8) ma^εan biziyaara(ti) hayy(in) min 'aḥyaa'i l-madeena

Ahmad turning to Jack

English : After that, we'll make (8) a tour together of a section (from among the sections) of the city.

NOTES

1 Notice that the verb precedes the subject ("Comes in Ahmad's wife"). This is the traditional structure of an Arabic sentence (which the influence of foreign languages and of popular dialects is tending to undermine.) **When the verb comes first, it is always in the singular** ; but it agrees with its subject in gender.

2 We have already seen (in Lesson 15, Note 3) the words for "girl", **bint** بِنْت as opposed to "boy", **walad** وَلَد ; and for "daughter", **'ibna(tun)**, as opposed to "son", **'ibn(un)**. But notice again the disappearance of the 'i at the beginning of these words when it is preceded by a vowel, as it is here. The same principle applies to the 'a of **'al** ("the") and to the 'i of **ism** ("name") and of **'ithnaani** ("two").

3 "As for..., he is playing". This is a very common turn of speech in Arabic. "As for" is **'amma** أَمَّا . The phrase that follows is always introduced by the "particle" **fa** فَ , which might be translated as : "well,..." and which is attached *either* (a) to the object-pronoun ("him" or "her") that acts as the expressed subject of the verb *or* (b) to the verb itself, whose form contains an implied pronoun. For example :

(a) As for..., **well, he... well, she...**
    'amma... fahuwa... fahiya   أَمَّا... فَهُوَ... فَهِيَ

(b) As for..., **well, (he) is playing...**
    'amma... fayalᶜab...   أَمَّا... فَيَلْعَب

4 Don't let the **aan** in **jeeraan(un)** جِيرَان lead you astray. This word is simply the plural of **jaar(un)** جَار , meaning "neighbour". The resemblance with the "dual" ending -aan(i) which we will look at in a moment, is purely coincidental.

5 We have referred from time to time to "dual" forms (used for **two** people or things) and have promised to come back to them. Here we are. Notice how "I'll see them both" is written : sa'araahuma سَأَرَاهُمَا

Here are the other dual pronoun forms :

You [normal plural]	'antum	أَنْتُمْ
You two	'antuma	أَنْتُمَا
They [normal plural]	hum	هُمْ
They two [both of them]	huma	هُمَا

254

The same principle applies to the other **subject-pronouns.** And the attached **object-pronouns** behave in the same way : **kum** becomes **kuma** and so on.

As for **nouns,** their dual endings are -aani in the subject case, -ayni in the object/adverb and oblique cases.

Now we will look at dual **verbs.**

(a) In the **pending aspect,** their characteristic ending is -aan أَن . Whereas "You want", in the normal plural, is tureedoon(a) تُرِيدُونَ

it becomes, in the dual, tureedaan(i) تُرِيدَانِ . The normal plural of "They want" is yureedoon(a) يُرِيدُونَ ; the dual is yureedaan(i) يُرِيدَانِ . (It should be mentioned that the n of this ending falls away when the verb is in the subjunctive or the jussive mood.)

(b) In the **completed** aspect, the characteristic dual ending is 'alif اَ .

You [plural] opened	fataḥtum	فَتَحْتُمْ
You [two] opened	fataḥtuma	فَتَحْتُمَا
They [plural] opened	fataḥu	فَتَحُوا
They [two] opened	fataḥa	فَتَحَا

6 The Arabic word for "some" is ba‘d بَعْض . As in English, depending on whether it is followed by a singular or a plural noun, it may mean either "a little (of something) or "several" (things). Whether singular or plural, it forms a yoked couple (like "pack of cigarettes") with the definite noun that follows it, which is necessarily in the oblique case, containing "of". Here are some examples :

In the singular, meaning "some" or "a little" :

A little (of) noise   ba$^\epsilon$du d-dajeej   بعضُ الضّجيج

Some (of) thing   ba$^\epsilon$da sh-shay'   بعضَ الشّيءِ

A little (of) time   ba$^\epsilon$da l-waqt   بعضَ الوقت

In the plural, meaning "a few" or "several" :

A few (of) sections (of town)   ba$^\epsilon$du l-'ahyaa'   بعضُ الأحياء

Some (of) cakes   ba$^\epsilon$du l-halawiyaat   بعضُ الحلويات

or :   ba$^\epsilon$du l-halwa   بعضُ الحلوى

Several (of) offices   ba$^\epsilon$du l-makaatib   بعضُ المكاتب

7 As you have just seen, "cakes" may be expressed either with the plural word, **halawiyaat** حلويات   or with the collective word, **halwa** حلوى

8 See the note on this verb on the next page.

EXERCISES

١ـ لا أُحبّ أن يلعبَ الأولادُ في الشّارع

1 I don't like the children to play (that the children play) in the street.

٢ـ سنقدّمُ لكم أولادَنا في مناسبةٍ أخرى

2 We will introduce (to you) our children on another occasion.

256

ـ هل تريـد أن تقومَ بزيارةِ البستان
بعد زيارةِ البيت ؟

3 Do you want to make a tour of the garden after visiting
(the visit of) the house ?

ـ مع من جئتَ ؟

4 With whom did you come ?

ـ وصلنا معًا من فرنسا بالطّائرة

5 We arrived together from France by plane.

ـ كيف حالُ العائلة ؟

6 How is (the state of) the family ?

GRAMMAR : verbs

The **indicative**, in the **pending aspect**, of two common verbs.

PLAY (la$^\epsilon$iba) (Root : L-$^\epsilon$-B)

I play	'al$^\epsilon$abu	ألعب
You [masc.] play	tal$^\epsilon$abu	تلعب
You [fem.] play	tal$^\epsilon$abeena	تلعبين
He plays	yal$^\epsilon$abu	يلعب
She plays	tal$^\epsilon$abu	تلعب

DO or CARRY OUT (qaama +bi) (Root : Q-W-M)

Remark : This very common verb has almost as many uses (and
possible translations) as our English verb "do". With it you can
make a tour, *pay* a visit, *perform* a role, *do* a job, *accomplish*
a task, *carry out* an action, etc. In the officialese of press releases,
it is used to *effect* a change of policy, *lodge* a complaint, and so on.

I do	'aqoomu bi	أقومُ بِ
You [masc.] do	taqoomu bi	تقومُ بِ
He does	yaqoomu bi	يقومُ بِ
Etc.		

الدَّرسُ الأربعون

'ad-darsu l-'arbaᶜoon

عند أحمد

١- من أين تريد أن نذهبَ ؟

٢- لا أدري^① ... لا أعرف

مدينتكم

٣- يمكن أن نقومَ بجولةٍ^②

في الحيّ حتّى حديقةِ

المدينة ؛ ما رأيُك !

258

The lesson the fortieth

Pronounce : ^ϵinda 'ahmad
English : In Ahmad's house (at Ahmad's)

1 'ahmad 'ila Jaak

Ahmad to Jack

Pronounce : min 'ayna tureed 'an nadhhaba ?
English : Which way do you want us to that we go ?

2 Jaak

Jack

Pronounce : la 'adri (1)...la 'a^ϵrif madeenatakum
English : I don't know (1)... I don't know your city.

3 'ahmad

Ahmad

Pronounce : yumkin 'an naqooma bijawla(tin) (2) fi l-hayy hatta hadeeqati l-madeena ; ma ra'yuk ?
English : We could (it is possible that we) make a tour around here (in this quarter), as far as the city park. What do you think ?

259

٤ ـ موافق !

٥ ـ نأخذُ السَّيّارة أم نذهب
مشيًا(٣)؟

٦ ـ مشيًا ، أحسنُ(٤) !

اللّـه(٥) ! هذا الشَّاي ممتاز !

٧ ـ هل تسمحُ لي بقليلٍ
منَ الحلوى بالعسل ؟

٨ ـ تفضّل ، يا أخي ! أنت
في بيتِك

٩ ـ والآن ... ما رأيُك لو
خرجنا(٦)؟

١٠ ـ مدينتُنا هي الأخرى(٧)
تنتظرُك بفارغِ الصَّبر

4   Jaak   *Pronounce* : muwaafiq

       Jack   *English* : Fine (I agree).

5   'aḥmad   *Pronounce* : na'khudhu s-sayyaara 'am nadhhab mashyan (3) ?

       Ahmad   *English* : Shall we take the car or go on foot (3) ?

6   Jaak   *Pronounce* : mashyan, 'aḥsan (4)... 'allaah ! (5)... haadha sh-shaay mumtaaz !

       Jack   *English* : On foot (is) better (4)... Lord (5) (but) this tea (is) good (excellent) !

7   Jaak   *Pronounce* : hal tasmaḥ li biqaleel(in) mina l-ḥalwa bil-$^{\epsilon}$asal ?

       Jack   *English* : May I have (do you allow me) a little honey-cake ?

8   'aḥmad   *Pronounce* : tafaḍḍal, ya 'akhi ! 'anta fi baytik

       Ahmad   *English* : Please help yourself, my friend (brother). Make yourself at home (you are in your house).

9   'aḥmad   *Pronounce* : wal-'aan... ma ra'yuk law kharajna ? (6)

       Ahmad   *English* : And now... What about going out (What would you think if we went out) (6) ?

10   'aḥmad   *Pronounce* : madeenatuna hiya l-'ukhra (7) tantaziruk bifaarighi ṣ-ṣabr

       Ahmad   *English* : Our town, too (7) is waiting for you with impatience.

NOTES

1 We saw in Lesson 32, Note 5, the up-in-the-air "I don't know",
la 'adri لا أُدري . Here is another example of it, followed by
the down-to-earth "I don't know" (*someone* or *something*),
la 'a^erif(u) لا أعرف .

2 And here is another example of the verb **qaama** plus the preposition **bi** (= he did, he made, etc.), whose forms and uses we
studied in Lesson 39. In the pending aspect, it is **yaqoomu** (= he
does, he makes.) And in this sentence, we see it with the **-a** ending
of the subjunctive mood, **naqooma** (= "that we make") :

(That) we make a tour	('an) naqooma bijawla(tin)
	نقوم بجولة
We make a tour	naqoom(u) biziyaara(tin)
	نقوم بزيارة

The two different words used for "tour" or "visit" are more or less
synonymous ; but the first one has the more general sense of "take
a look around" or "go for a walk", while the second one means
more specifically "visit a place" or "pay a visit to someone".

3 The Arabic word that we have translated as "on foot",
mashyan مشيا in fact means "walking". It is a verbal noun
whose subject-case form is **mashyun** مشي . (It here has
the adverbial ending **-an** because it has an adverbial function :
it says *how*.) The verbal noun is derived from the verb
masha مشى ("he walked"), whose pending aspect ("he
walks"), is **yamshi** يمشي .

4 "Better", **'ahsan** أحسن . The comparative is formed in
the same way as the superlative, which we saw in Lesson 38, Note 6.
But, as in English, it has no definite article ("good - better - *the*
best").

5 "Lord", **'allaah** الله! is again used here exactly as it would
be in English, as an exclamation of pleasure. See Lesson 30, Note 4.

6 The literal sense of **ma ra'yuk ?** is "What is your opinion ?"
As for **law** لو , it means "if". The combination of the two is
always followed by a **verb in the completed aspect** : "What would

262

you think if we **went** out". Other examples of this are :

... if we went	... law dhahabna	لو ذهبنا
... if we ate	... law 'akalna	لو أكلنا
... if we drank	... law sharibna	لو شربنا

The word for "if", **law** is also used to express *unlikely suppositions:* "If I had wings, I would fly". But, in Arabic, *both* the verbs of this sentence are put in the **completed aspect** : "If I had wings, I flew." The supposition is expressed as if it were an accomplished fact. You see why we say that verbs have a completed aspect rather than a past tense.)

7 The expression **hiya l-'ukhra** هي الأخرى means literally : "it the other". It is often used as another way of saying "also" or "likewise" : **'aydan** or **kaadhaalik** أيضاً ـ كذلك

The gender both of the pronoun and of the adjective that make up this expression has to agree with the gender of what the expression applies to ; whereas **'aydan** and **kaadhaalik** are invariable. Here are examples of both ways of saying "also" with feminine and with masculine words :

Feminine

The town also :

> **'al madeena 'aydan** المدينة أيضاً

> **'al madeena hiya l-'ukhra** المدينة هي الأخرى

Masculine

The office also :

> **'al maktab 'aydan** المكتب أيضاً

> **'al maktab huwa l-'aakhar** المكتب هو الآخر

EXERCISES

١- متى تبدأ عملك في المكتب ؟

1 When do your start (your) work at the office ?

٢- لا أُدري من أَيـن أَبـدأُ

2 I don't know where to begin (from where I begin).

٣- هل تسمح لي بأن أصحبك
إلى المطار ؟

3 May I (do you allow me to) accompany you to the airport ?

٤- يسرّني أن نقومَ بجولةٍ معًا

4 I'd be glad to (that we) make a tour together.

٥- هل أنت موافق أم لا ؟

5 Do you agree or not ?

٦- هل نريد أن تقومَ بجولةٍ مشيًا
أم تفضّل أن تذهبَ بالسّيارةِ ؟

6 Do you want to (that you) make a tour on foot (walking) or do you prefer to go by (the) car ?

٧- هو مِشغول ؛ لا يمكن أن يتغدّى
معك اليوم

7 He is busy ; he can't (it is not possible that he) have lunch with you today.

264

٨ ـ إعمل كما تحبّ : فبيتي بيتُك

8   Do as you like : my house is yours.

٩ ـ خرج قبلَ عشر دقائق

9   He went out ten minutes ago.

١٠ ـ ما رأيُك لو دخلنا البيت ؟

10   What about going into the house (what would you think if we went into the house) ?

من أين تريد أن نبدأ ؟

عند أحمد

١- إلى اللِّقاء ، يا سيِّدتي ،
و شكرًا على حرارة اسْتِقبالِكمْ ⓵

٢- إلى اللِّقاء ، يا أُنْستي ...
شكرًا على الشَّاي : كان لذيذٌ

٣- ما شربتُ أطيبَ ⓸ منه
قطُّ ⓷

٤- إلى اللِّقاء قريبًا ، ⓸
إن شاءَ اللّـهُ !

(يخرجان و ⓹ قد وصل الولدانِ
الأصغران)

266

The lesson the first and the fortieth

Pronounce : ^ϵinda 'aḥmad
English : In Ahmad's house (at Ahmad's)

1 Jaak 'ila
zawja(ti)
'aḥmad
Jack to
Ahmad's
wife

Pronounce : 'ila l-liqaa', ya sayyidati
washukran ^ϵala ḥaraarati stiqbaalikum (1)

English : Good-bye, Madame, and thank
you for your [plur.] friendly reception
(for the warmth of your reception) (1).

2 Jaak 'ila
faatima
Jack to
Faatima

Pronounce : 'ila l-liqaa', ya 'aanisati...
shukran ^ϵala sh-shaay ; kaana ladheedh(an)

English : Good-bye, Miss... thank you for
the tea ; it was delicious.

3 Jaak 'ila
faatima
Jack to
Fatima

Pronounce : ma sharibtu 'aṭyab (2)
minhu qaṭṭu (3)

English : I've never (3) drunk any better
(2) (than it).

4 Jaak 'ila
muḥammad
Jack to
Muhammad

Pronounce : 'ila l-liqaa' qareeban (4)
'in shaa'a l-llaah

English : Good-bye, and I hope to see
you soon (4).

(yakhrujaan waqad (5) waṣala l-waladaani l-'aṣgharaani)
(The two of them go out just as (5) the two younger boys
arrive.)

٥ - أه! ها هو عبدُ اللّطيف

مع ابني الأصغر: مهدي

٦ - صباحَ الخيرِ، يا عبدُ اللّطيف!

كم عمرُك؟

٧ - عشر سنوات ⑥

٨ - وأنت يا مهدي؟

٩ - ستّ سنوات

١٠ - إبنُكَ الأصغر لطيفٌ جدًّا!

أمّا الآخر فهو أيضًا جميل!

١١ - عائلتُك لطيفة، يا أحمد!

مبروك! ⑦

5 'aḥmad
Ahmad

Pronounce : 'aah ! ha huwa [€]abdu l-lateef
maᵉa bni l-'aṣghar, mahdi

English : Ah ! here (comes) Abdul Latif
with my youngest son, Mahdi.

6 Jaak 'ila
[€]abdi
l-lateef
Jack to
Abdul
Latif

Pronounce : ṣabaaḥa l-khayr, ya [€]abda
l-lateef. kam ᵉumruk ?

English : Good afternoon, Abdul Latif.
How old are you ?

7 [€]abdu
l-lateef
Abdul
Latif

Pronounce : ᵉashar sanawaat (6)

English : Ten years (6).

8 Jaak 'ila
mahdi
Jack to
Mahdi

Pronounce : wa'anta, ya mahdi ?

English : And you, Mahdi ?

9 mahdi
Mahdi

Pronounce : sitt(u) sanawaat(in)

English : Six years.

10 Jaak 'ila
'aḥmad
Jack to
Ahmad

Pronounce : 'ibnuka l-aṣghar lateef(un)
jiddan ; 'amma l-'aakhar fahuwa 'aydan
jameel !

English : Your youngest son is very
nice-looking ; as for the other, he too
is handsome.

11 Jaak 'ila
'aḥmad
Jack to
Ahmad

Pronounce : ᵉaa'ilatuk lateefa, ya 'aḥmad!
mabrook (7) !

English : You have a fine family (your
family is beautiful), Ahmad ! Congratulations (7) !

١٢ ـ شُكْرًا، وَلِلّٰهِ الْحَمْدُ ⑧

١٣ ـ لِنَخْرُجِ الْآنَ ! ⑨

**

NOTES

1 The word 'istiqbaal إِسْتِقْبَال is another verbal noun, Its literal sense is "welcoming" or "receiving". It is derived from the verb 'istaqbala ("he welcomed"), whose pending aspect is yastaqbilu ("he welcomes"). All verbs that begin with 'ist make verbal nouns on the same model as the present one ; we will look at them more closely later on. Notice the disappearrance of 'i after a word ending in a vowel.

2 This is our first encounter with the comparative "better *than*", 'atyab min أَطْيَب مِنْ . The word for "better", 'atyab, is the comparative of "good", tayyib ; while min is here used to mean "than", to which "it", hu, is attached. When used in combination with min, the comparative adjective is invariable (neither its number nor its gender changes). Here are a few more examples :

Big	kabeer	Bigger	'akbar	Bigger than	'akbar min
Small	sagheer	Smaller	'asghar	Smaller than	'asghar min
Much	katheeran	More	'akthar	More than	'akthar min

3 We saw in Lesson 22, Note 3, the word for "never" that is used when the verb is in the **pending aspect** : 'abadan أَبَدًا .
But when the verb is in the **completed aspect**, as it is here, "never" becomes "not...ever", ma plus qattu قَطّ , with the verb in the middle.

4 The word used for "soon" is qareeban قَرِيبًا , which expresses proximity in time as well as in space ("near by"). Notice the adverbial ending, -an.

5 We have seen wa until now as the general conjunction, "and". But when it is used as it is here—that is, (a) joined to qad and (b) followed by a verb in the completed aspect — it takes on the specific sense of "just as" or "at the moment when".

270

12   'aḥmad   *Pronounce* : shukran, wali-llaah(i) l-ḥamd (8)

     Ahmad   *English* : Thank you, and Allah be praised (8) !

13   'aḥmad   *Pronounce* : linakhruji (9) l-'aan !

     Ahmad   *English* : Let's go out (9) now.

✱✱

6 "Years", **sanawaat** سنوات is the plural of **sana(tun)** سنة . We will see later the principle behind the formation of such plurals.

7 This way of saying "Congratulations !" — **mabrook** — مبروك — means literally, "May you be blessed" or "Blessings on you". It is generally used for occasions such as weddings and birthdays. Congratulations of a less ceremonious kind (on getting a promotion, a raise, a good job, etc.) are expressed with **tahni'a** [singular] or **tahaanin** [plural] تهانٍ تهنئة .

8 This formula, **li-llaah(i) l-ḥamd** للّه الحمد , which we have translated as "Allah be praised", means literally, "To Allah the praise". It is just an upside-down version of the formula that you already know, '**al ḥamdu li-llaah** الحمد للّه .

9 We saw in Lesson 8, Note 2, that the "chopped-off" jussive mood of the verb is used as an imperative for the first and third persons : "Let's..." or "May he..." The imperative sense of the verb is here reinforced by prefixing to it **li** لِ . An alternative prefix that does the same job is **hayya** هَيّا . For example :

Let's take   **lina'khudh**   لِنَأْخُذ

    or :   **hayya na'khudh**   هَيّا نَأْخُذ

271

EXERCISES

١- لن أبقى هناك أكثر من ربع ساعة

1 I won't stay there more than a quarter of an hour.

٢- هل هو أصغر الأولاد

2 Is he the youngest child (of the children) ?

٣- بيتكم أوسع من بيتنا

3 Your [plur.] house (is) roomier than ours (than our house).

٤- إبني أصغر من إبنك

4 My son (is) younger than yours (than your son).

٥- كم عمر إبنتك الكبرى ؟

5 How old is your eldest daughter ?

٦- عمرها : خمس عشرة سنة

6 She is fifteen (her age is fifteen years).

٧- هل رأيت مدينة أجمل من هذه ؟

7 Have you seen a more beautiful city than this ?

272

٨ - هل تكونُ في الفندق لاستقبالِنا ؟

8   Will you be at the hotel to receive us (for receiving us) ?

٩ - أنا تَعبان أكثر منك

9   I am more tired than you.

١٠ - هذه الزّهورُ الحمراء تعجبُني ؛
إنّها أجمل من البيضاء

10   I like these red flowers (these red flowers please me) ;
they are prettier than the white (ones).

شكراً على حرارة استقبالِكم !

273

الدَّرسُ الثَّاني و الأُربعون

'ad-darsu th-thaani wal'arba^عoon

مراجعة

This is our last review lesson before going on to the second volume of the ASSIMIL Arabic course. We will use it to say a bit more about points that have come up in the lessons just preceding and to take a much closer look at a basic principle of the Arabic language — the forming of words from consonant roots, vowel patterns, adders and inserts — which we first brought up in the Introduction and which we have dealt with intermittently throughout the book.

1 The comparative and superlative of adjectives

In Lesson 41, Note 2, we saw some typical comparatives, such as "bigger" from "big" and "smaller" from "small". You probably noticed that they were formed not by the addition of an ending comparable to the English "-er" but by a change in the **internal structure** of the words themselves — more precisely, in their vowel patterns. The vowel pattern of "big", **kabeer,** and of "small", **sagheer,** is **a-ee.** That of "bigger", **'akbar,** and of "smaller", **'asghar,** is **'a-a.** This pattern is used both for comparatives and for superlatives ("the biggest", "the smallest"). But, as we shall see in a moment, *feminine* superlatives of adjectives — which are rarely used — have the vowel pattern **u-a.** We will look first at comparatives, then at superlatives.

The lesson the second and the fortieth

Pronounce : muraaja^εa
English : Review

(a) Comparatives. The only special feature of these that needs to be pointed out is that they are always used in their **masculine singular form only** : they don't change at all in accordance with the gender and number of the nouns they qualify. The word for "bigger" is the same in "a bigger boy" as in "bigger girls". As for "than", it is simply **min.** Here are a couple of examples :

My car [feminine] (is) smaller than his car.

sayyaarati **'asghar** min sayyaaratihi

This office [masculine] (is) smaller than my office.

haadha l-maktab **'asghar** min maktabi

For future reference, we should mention here a grammatical peculiarity of comparatives. While they have the normal case endings, **-u, -a,** and **-i** when *definite,* their *indefinite* case endings deviate from the rules in two ways : (1) they have no final **-n,** and (2) there are only two of them — **-u** for the subject case and **-a** for both the object/adverb and the oblique cases. For this reason, they are called "diptotes".

(b) Superlatives. The word for "bigg**est**" is the same as the word for "bigg**er**", **'akbar** ; but when it has a superlative sense it is used in different ways — three different ways, to be precise :

The first (and preferred) way to use it is illustrated by the following sentences :

The biggest (one) of hotels	**'akbaru l-fanaadiq(i)**
The roomiest (one) of cars	**'awsa$^\epsilon$u s-sayyaaraat(i)**

Notice here (1) that the superlative becomes a **noun** ; (2) that it is followed by another noun — **definite,** in the **plural** and in the **oblique case,** containing "of" ; and (3) that is does not itself have the definite article, **'al,** which we would expect. Why not ? Because, as you will at once recognize, the two nouns assembled in this way form a "yoked couple", on the same model as "pack of cigarettes". You will also remember that, in a "yoked couple", since the first word is *made* definite by the word that follows it and pins it down, it doesn't need to be further tagged as a definite noun by **'al.**

Now, in the above two sentences, the superlatives, "the biggest" and "the roomiest" are what we might call "absolute" — they are superlatives "in the air". But Arabic has a simple way of making them less absolute — of bringing them down to earth by placing them within a specific frame of reference. For example :

276

The biggest hotel *in the city*	'akbar(u) funduq(in) fi l-madeena
The most beautiful city *in the world*	'ajmal(u) madeena fi l-ᵉaalam

Notice what has happened here : **funduq(in)** and **madeena** have become **singular** ; and, though again in the **oblique case**, the case ending is the one for **indefinite** nouns. But we still have a "yoked couple".

The third way to use a superlative adjective is to treat it as if it were a normal descriptive (or qualifying) adjective, like "green" or "unhappy". When it is used in this way, it *behaves* like a normal adjective : it agrees in gender and number with its noun, and it has the definite article :

In the biggest hotel [masc.]	fi l-funduq(i) l-'akbar
He (is) the smallest	huwa l-'aṣghar
She (is) the smallest	hiya ṣ-ṣughra
The biggest cities [fem.]	'al mudunu l-kubra

In the last two examples, we have used the feminine forms of **'aṣghar : ṣughra**, and of **'akbar : kubra**. Both have the **u-a** vowel pattern mentioned earlier. But the fact is that very few adjectives are used in their feminine superlative forms ; and the adjective construction in general, for superlatives, is less used than one or the other of the "yoked couple" constructions dealt with above, in which the superlative itself, used as a noun, is always masculine, regardless of the gender of the word it is yoked to.

277

2 The Comparative of Adverbs

We have seen that adjectives (which normally modify *nouns*) can be made to act as adverbs (which normally modify *verbs*) if we simply give them an adverb-case ending. For example :

qaleel (few, little, slight)	qaleelan (slightly)	قَلِيلٌ
katheer (numerous, abundant)	katheeran (abundantly)	كَثِيرًا
ḥasan (good)	ḥasanan (well)	حَسَنًا

As in English, the comparatives of adverbs are often indistinguishable from those of the corresponding adjectives : "I have *less whisky*", "I drink *less*". Or : "There is *better swimming* here", "I swim *better*". You will find these indistinguishable comparatives in such adverbial expressions as :

(I swim) less than...	'aqall min	أَقَلُّ مِن
(I swim) more than...	'akthar min	أَكْثَرُ مِن
(I swim) better than...	'aḥsan min	أَحْسَنُ مِن

3 Verb families, their members, their offshoots

(a) **Families and their members.** We have said that Arabic verbs are designated not by their infinitive ("to know"), which does not exist in Arabic, but by the completed aspect form ("he knew"), in which the three-consonant root of the verb most clearly appears ; and we have indicated, for each verb studied, its root. The root of a verb (or of any other word in Arabic) expresses a general concept — in this instance, the concept of "knowing".

In the simplest (or "first") form of a verb — "he knew" — the **ROOT** is completed (or "filled out", so that it can be pronounced) by a **PATTERN** made up just of unwritten short vowels. Here are a few examples of verbs in their "first" or "naked" forms :

He went out	**KHaRaJa**	خرج
He entered	**DaKHaLa**	دخل
He sat down	**JaLaSa**	جلس

From the first forms of verbs are derived others, customarily numbered from 2 to 10, which extend or modify or (to use the Arabic term) "augment" the meaning of the first one. Very few verbs have all the so-called "derived forms" from 2 to 10 ; some have only a couple of them ; and some have no first form at all, their additional forms being derived rather from a noun — "it rained" from "the rain". But, in general, the series made up of a verb's first form and of the various other forms derived from it constitute what may be called a "family" of verbal meanings.

Suppose we look at the second forms of a few common verbs and see how they are derived from the first forms :

1 He broke   **KaSaRa**

2 He smashed to pieces   **KaSSaRa**

1 He preceded   **QaDiMa**

2 He caused to precede (hence : presented, offered, served)   **QaDDaMa**

| 1 | He knew | ^εaLiMa |

1 He knew   ^εaLiMa

2 He caused to know (hence : taught)   ^εaLLaMa

As you see at once, what has been done in all these examples is to **double the second consonant of the root**. (In Arabic script, this is done by placing a **shadda** over it.) This is the identifying mark of a verb's second form. And what all second forms further have in common is that each "augments" the meaning of its corresponding first form by **intensifying** it or by adding to it a sense of **repetition** or of **causation**.

Other "derived forms", numbered from 3 to 10, are obtained by acting on the root in other ways — but in a specific and invariable way for each of the numbered forms, and with a specific kind of change in meaning for each.

The other **ways** of acting on the root consist just of

(a) **inserting** a letter (a consonant or a long vowel) between consonants of the root ;
(b) **prefixing** a letter or a syllable ; or
(c) **both**.

من أين تريد أن نبدأ ؟

As for the **kinds** of change in meaning that take place between the first form of a verb and each of its derived forms, these too are perfectly systematic and uniform ; but we will reserve the description and analysis of them for the second volume of this book.

You are already familiar with a number of verbs in their derived forms. Here are some of them, in which we call your attention by capitals to the identifying marks of each derived form number :

Verb	Root	Form Number	Procedure
'Aḥdara (he brought)	Ḥ-D-R	4	Prefix 'A
TA^عaLLama (he learned)	ع-L-M	5	Prefix TA Shadda
TAshaRRafa (he was honored)	SH-R-F	5	Prefix TA Shadda
'inTabaha (he was careful)	N-B-H	8	Insert T and prefix 'i if word is not preceded by a vowel
'inTaẓara (he was waited for)	N-Ẓ-R	8	Same as above
'iSTaqbala (he received, welcomed)	Q-B-L	10	Prefix ST (itself preceded by 'i if there is no other vowel before it)

(b) Offshoots. We have seen that, starting from a basic three-consonant root, we obtain a first-form verb ; and that, starting from the first-form verb, we obtain, by inserting or by adding letters, up to nine variations or shades of meaning related to that of the first. Now we will go one step further.

From any one of these ten forms of a verb, we can in turn derive — again in a rigorously systematic way for each form (with one small exception)— various "parts of speech" other than verbs properly speaking. We will stick for the moment to just two : the **active participle** (which, you will remember, does various jobs in Arabic) and the **verbal noun** (some of whose many uses you have also encountered).

We will start with a first-form verb, ^ε**alima** عَلِمَ whose meaning is "he knew" and whose consonant root is ^ε**-L-M.**

Its **active participle,** "knowing" — hence "one who knows": a scholar, a scientist — is ^ε**aalim** عَالِم . We obtain this active participle by adding to the basic root, ^ε-L-M, the vowel pattern, **AA-I.** (We saw other examples of this in the Introduction, page XLII : "writing-writer", "working-worker", etc.)

From the same primary verb we obtain a **verbal noun** — "the fact of knowing", hence "knowledge" or "science" — which is ^ε**ilm** عِلْم . We do so in this instance just by (a) stripping the root bare and (b) inserting a short vowel after its first consonant. (However, this is the exceptional case referred to above : verbal nouns derived from Form 1 verbs are irregular ; they have various patterns.)

282

Now we will go on to some verbs in derived form number 2, starting with the second form of "he knew", ᶜalima عَلِمَ which is "he caused repeatedly to know" — hence "he taught" — ᶜallama عَلَّمَ .

To obtain the **active participle** of a second-form verb, we (a) add to it the prefix **mu** and (b) apply the vowel pattern **A-I**. We thus come up with muᶜallim مُعَلِّم "teaching" — hence "one who teaches" : teacher, professor.

To obtain the **verbal noun** — "the fact of teaching", hence "education" — from the same second-form verb, we (a) add the prefix **ta** and (b) insert **EE** after the second consonant of the root. And we come up with taᶜleem تَعْلِيم .

Applying the same procedures to a couple of other second-form verbs with different roots :

1 **Root** : GH-Y-R (Concept : "otherness". [Remember ghayr, "other than"]).

   Form 2 of verb, with second consonant doubled : ghayyara غَيَّرَ "he made different" : changed, altered.

   Active participle : mughayyir مُغَيِّر , "changing" — hence : "one who changes [something]" : changer.

   Procedure : prefix **mu**, apply vowel pattern **A-I**.

   Verbal noun : taghyeer تَغْيِير , "the fact of changing" [something], hence a change (of policy, for example).

   Procedure : prefix **ta**, insert **EE** after second consonant of root.

2 Root : D-KH-N (Concept : "smoke" or "smokiness")

Form 2 of verb, with second consonant doubled :

dakhkhana دَخَّنَ , "he caused to give off smoke, or expelled smoke" — hence smoked (a pipe, a cigarette).

Active participle : mudakhkhin مُدَخِّن , "smoking" — hence "one who smokes" : smoker. Procedure : prefix **mu**, apply vowel patter A-I.

Verbal noun : tadkheen تَدْخِين , "the fact of smoking" — hence : "smoking (as used in "No smoking allowed").

Procedure : prefix **ta**, insert **EE** after second consonant of root.

Although we will not study in the present volume derived forms of verbs (and their offshoots) beyond the second, it will probably please you to know that you are already familiar with more of them than you realized. Here are some verbal nouns obtained from **third-form** verbs :

Verb	Root	Meaning
musaa$^\epsilon$ada(tun)	S-$^\epsilon$-D	the fact of helping : help
mumaarasa(tun)	M-R-S	the fact of exercising : practice
mukhaabara(tun)	KH-B-R	the fact of calling : a call
muraaja$^\epsilon$a(tun)	R-J-$^\epsilon$	the fact of reviewing : review

The "procedure", in this instance, is : prefix **mu** and apply the vowel pattern **AA-A** plus a feminine ending in **taa' marboota**.

Any resemblance that you have noted in all the above to a child's game of construction is not coincidental. We bring up the whole matter at this point, before you go on to Volume 2, so that you will be aware of the immense range of words to which the Arabic system of word formation, applied to the relatively small number of words that you have learned until now, gives you access. The game of construction (to push the image further) enables you to make fire-engines, wind-mills and skyscrapers with the same set of pieces.

INDEX

This is an index of subjects and of words that are discussed in the book. It is not a general vocabulary. Words are distinguished from subjects by *italics*. They are given in English and in English alphabetical order, followed by their transcribed Arabic equivalents, in **bold-face** type.

A certain number of Arabic words that have no English equivalents or that you would otherwise not know how to look for are also listed in bold-face type.

287

Composition et Mise en page
INTER-SERVICE EDITIONS
419.24.30

Time - 244
Telephone 202
#s 77, 95-97, 116-117
week days 110
like, as, p 198
let's 271

L'impression de ce livre
a été réalisée sur les presses
des Imprimeries Aubin
à Poitiers/Ligugé

pour les Éditions Assimil

Achevé d'imprimer en mars 1985
N° d'édition, 736 — N° d'impression, L 19665
Dépôt légal, mars 1985

Reliure par la SIRC à Marigny-le-Châtel

negatives - p 216-218, 270

past 219

Imprimé en France

1. On the airplane - no smoking, tell time
2. " " " polite phrases, please, thanks, prefer
do you have. Acc. case
3 " " " beverages. 上 lè
4 " " " Qs - occupation, excuse-me. What time is it
9. 5 " Where is? What is wrong w. you? Headache
23 6 " " " Do you arrive soon? what's your name? pronouns
29. Review
38. 8. At the airport. Weather. ; 15. Landing card
subjunctive
Lặ (Let's) + jussive
42.9. " " Family, name, date & place of birth
address, profession, nationality
colors - p44.
47. 10. " " Customs. Anything to declare?
passport
51. 11. " " " "
55. 12. " " " Exchange Office , Right, Left - 58
subjunctive
60. 13. " " " Directions
66 14 Review
72. 15. At the hotel _ Ride in car. How many children?
married/single
78. 16. " " " " future or órósò. Speak well
understand
84 17 " " " Talk about room
90. 18 " " porter to room, tip #s
98 19 " " In the room, bed, bathroom
tired, rest

140 Directions (#25)

154 Restaurant (#27)

262 33 Telephone
216 negatives
224 36 Taxsi

240 38 At Ahmad's   (244 TIME)
246 w/o لا يوجد
250 39 " " Intro to Family

40

270   Let's | ل + jussive | or لِنا

Never: imperfect لم / Perfect لمّا لم ب